Parenting Day by Day
365 Tips for Raising Bright and Goal Driven Kids

Dr. Nicoline Ambe
www.nicolineambe.com

DEDICATION

I dedicate this book to all courageous moms and dads who dedicate their lives to authentically and consciously raise smart and goal driven children. I honor and salute you! This book is also written in loving memory of my husband, a wonderful father who loved his children!

JOIN OUR VIP CLUB!
Get a free Giveaway!

ACKNOWLEDGMENTS

I want to thank all my readers and those who have purchased my books. I also thank those who have left reviews of my books on Amazon. Your positive reviews give me a reason to produce more quality content for parents. Again, THANK YOU!

Introduction

Parenting can be an uncertain and winding road. You set out on the journey with the best intentions of reaching a final destination. You do all you can to prepare for the journey, but somewhere along the way what you encounter may surprise you, excite you, or hurt you. That's right; parenting is synonymous with uncertainty. You may provide all that you can, emotionally and materially, for your children but who they ultimately become is not up to you; and it may or may not align with your vision. As a parent you just don't know how your children will turn out. You may do everything humanly possible to provide for them and still fall short, or exceed expectations. (I hope it's the latter).

This book, **Parenting Day by Day**, is a roadmap to best practices that give parents a little more predictability and certainty on the path to better parenting. As a parent of three children, I can attest that every parent wants to raise children who have control of their lives, who make smart, independent decisions, who are focused and goal driven, who can support themselves as adults, take care of their children, and prepare for their retirement future. This book is written with this basic premise in mind!

The book discusses 365 principles that parents can implement in their daily lives to raise children who are smart and goal driven. This is not a book that you can read in one sitting. It is suitable as a daily reference and reinforces practices that make you the parent you desire to be. So make it a goal to read one tip a day, every day. There is something for every parent in the book, no matter your race, educational background, gender or beliefs. If you successfully implement half of the principles in this book, you will be well on your way to a more predictable outcome on your parenting journey. You will live to see your children prosper and achieve their dreams!

Get your copy today, pull up your bootstraps, and let's hit the road...

1

1. You are Human, with Flaws

As a parent, there are times when you doubt whether you are doing a good job or whether your child will grow up to meet your expectations. The fear of failure is real for many parents. You need to remember you are human, and you have faults. You will try to do the best you can as a parent, but it may not always turn out the way you want. Let love and conscience be your guide as you give your child your best care. If you parent intentionally and consciously with love, you will make the best decisions humanly possible. Parenting with intention means that your words and actions are deliberately designed to produce positive results in your child. That is the least you can do, and when you do that, you can chalk up your errors to just being human.

2. Discover Abilities

One of the most powerful gifts you can give your child is discovering who they truly are, and what they are good at. What exactly is your child good at? What aspect of their personality makes them such an amazing person in your sight? What specific skills do they have? Your child's abilities are their unique selling points. It is their unique blueprint that differentiates them from others. Try to discover and nurture your child's unique abilities and their areas of strength, because this is what they will build on to create a successful future they love. More importantly, see your child the way God sees them, and you will make manifest the power that is within them.

3. Nourish Belief

Belief. A very powerful six-letter word. Without belief, your child may not have the courage to take action, especially action that moves them out of their comfort zone. Belief is the ability to trust yourself; to trust your talent, your instinct, your decisions, your opinions. Sadly, many people do not trust themselves. They doubt that their actions and words will be received favorably, so they act against their best interest by holding back. Teach your child to believe that they **can**, to believe in who they are, to believe that their views and actions have value. Teach them to trust themselves more, and to believe that who they are, and what they have to offer, adds value to the world.

4. Patience and Understanding

There is no denying children have annoying little ways that sometimes drive you crazy. You may often get irritated and upset when they play too much, break things around the house, scream, and yell, or just make poor choices. Be patient and understand it is part of growing up. We all make mistakes. Even as adults, we do things that annoy others. I am certain there are also things you do which annoy your child. Try to keep your child's annoying behaviors and actions in perspective. See it for what it is – the growing process. Take a different approach to dealing with it by finding practical and reasonable ways to help your child correct their actions. Help your child learn from their mistakes and discover the lesson in every circumstance. Trust me, the frustration you feel will soon be in the past!

5. Motivated about School

As human beings, we all need to be motivated at certain points in our lives, no matter how much discipline we have. The need for constant motivation is even greater in children. Motivation is enthusiasm to continue to pursue a goal, even when you do not feel like it, or even when a part of you wants to quit. Parents have a duty to encourage, empower, inspire, and uplift their children to have a positive outlook on life and school. You do this by being positive – using positive words and being positive in your actions. Be more of an encourager by helping your child see the good in school by painting a beautiful picture even while sharing some ugly truths. Let them know they can achieve their goals through hard work and receive rewards that will help them be a better human being.

6. Open Communication

Communication is a critical aspect of any relationship. Develop open lines of communication with your child so they can feel comfortable talking to you about anything. Avoid passing judgment on anything your child says or does because this will make them feel reticent about sharing aspects of their life with you. Be open. Listen more than you talk. Get the full story. Wait to be asked for your opinion and never blame your child without fully assessing the situation objectively. Watch your tone. Avoid screaming and yelling as a means of solving problems. Ask your child's opinion on issues. Improve on your receptive communication skills by making sure that you do not judge or place blame unnecessarily. When your child is talking to you, stop what you are doing and pay attention to them. Acknowledge their presence. When you make them feel like their voice counts, they will want to tell you more.

7. Live within Your Means

Most parents want the best for their children, and many even want their children to live a better life than they did. Others splurge on the finer things in life, even when they cannot afford it. They live extravagant lifestyles they cannot pay for and go into debt to purchase things they cannot afford for personal pleasure, aggrandizement, or to prove something to others. You cannot teach your child financial lessons if you do not have a grasp on your finances. If you are a financial train wreck, or if you consistently set a bad example, you are not only harming yourself, but you are also teaching your child to mismanage their money. This is dangerous! The problem with living beyond your means is you cannot help your child with college and wedding expenses, and if you do not save adequately for your retirement, your child may end up taking care of you. Live within your means!

8. Find Balance in Life

A hectic pace, noise, and clutter can sometimes get in the way of true living. Unplug from it all and find balance. Remember that every area of your life is crucial to finding happiness and fulfillment. Your health, spirituality, career, family, and social life are essential to living a full and balanced life. If your health is suffering, you will find it hard to give your family what they need. You will find it hard to reach your personal goals. If you are not spiritual, you will lose your sense of self and not be able to make informed decisions that positively impact your family. So, strive to maintain balance in your life by ensuring you practice habits which enhance and nurture your well-being and peace of mind. When you enjoy balance in your personal life, you will have more to give your child.

9. Multiple Personalities

Our children come in different shapes, sizes, abilities, skill levels, and personalities. No two children are the same. This is especially true for parents with specials needs children. The demands for dealing with children with multiple personalities and abilities can sometimes weigh on a parent. Be encouraged and strive to maintain your balance. Be organized so you can ease the transition between activities. Prioritize your time daily, and say no to activities that do not move you forward or which weigh you down. Develop a new mindset and a new way of seeing things. Take excellent care of your health, your mind, your spiritual life. Create a life which keeps you in control of your circumstances, so you are not darting from one activity to another, feeling flustered and overwhelmed.

10. Boost Self-Esteem

Self-esteem is a powerful attribute all parents must strive to inculcate in their children. It is certainly not easy to do this because we live in a world that can sometimes be negative. Sometimes this negativity is not intentional. It is just conforming to socially acceptable habits and values. How many times have you heard yourself telling your child, "No, you can't do that"? Each time you say that, you instill fear in your child; fear that something bad will happen. Your reactions are also coming from a place of fear. But over time, this affects your child because he begins to doubt himself, and wonders what he should or should not do. Help your children develop self-esteem by making them feel great about themselves. Make them feel empowered and capable by using positive and empowering words.

11. Save for Retirement

"Early" is the perfect time to start saving for retirement. What does this have to do with your parenting, you ask? Everything. Your ability to be self-sufficient during your retirement years will impact your child and your life. Make plans now to set money aside for your retirement. It is also a good habit to teach your child about effectively saving money. Many parents hope to live on social security, but as we know this is not sufficient to cover all of your food, bills, and other expenses during retirement. You want to have foresight, and be smart about ensuring that you set money aside to live comfortably, or at least without lack, in your retirement years. If not, you will be living on the good will of your children and the hope that they are nice enough to support you.

12. From Talent to Action

Your child has gifts and abilities that can simply blow you away. Many parents do not see the skills their children possess, and so they do not nourish and nurture those gifts. Take time in your child's life to look and to clearly see the gifts and talents which your child possesses. Find opportunities to expose them to various activities to see which ones they love. Once you discover your child's ability, think about how you can help them develop it. Turn it into strength; tell them about it. For example, say, "Jesse, you are a great artist. I love your painting." Or "Landry, I know you can achieve anything you set your mind to because you are very bold and determined."

13. Mental Health

The world is becoming an increasingly busy place with a much faster pace. Thanks to technological advances, there seem to be so many things to see and do, and children are exposed to more each day. This has the effect of causing children not just to be mentally busy with a lot to see and do, but it affects their values and beliefs because they are exposed to so much information from different sources. Help your child be mentally healthy by being "present" for them and with them. Show them genuine love and affection. Help them distinguish themselves from what is happening around them. Help them recognize their true selves – who they are. Help them love themselves more and act in their best interest. Being mentally healthy means showing them how **not** to have a bandwagon mentality, but to love themselves deeply enough to honor and follow their unique path in life.

14. Daily Conversations

What do you talk to your child about on a daily basis? Having real life conversations with your child is important. Discuss things that are happening in the news. Discuss the incidences in life that cause people to behave in a certain way. Ask their opinion on real life events. Ask them what happens at school on a daily basis. Talk to them about tolerance, courage, careers, how they see their life in the future. Discuss books you have read or books your child has read, and find meaning in the content of those books. Do not be the kind of parent who consistently passes judgment on their child, or who imposes their views on them. Be the kind of parent who influences in a positive and inspiring way. Be the kind of parent who is informed of what is happening and makes it a duty to share it with their child in a way that teaches life lessons and does not point fingers.

15. Develop their Capabilities

I will make a bold statement here: "Your child is far more capable than you believe." Every parent's first instinct is to rush to protect their children. No parent wants to see their child struggle or go through hard times. But the truth is that sometimes conflict helps your child become capable. It helps them develop resiliency, which is a powerful life skill. Life gets extremely tough at times, so you want to prepare your child for when things do not go their way, times when they will experience hardship. So strive to help your child develop their capabilities by pushing them to do more and give more. Encourage them to do some of those things that they do not feel like doing, like spending extra time reading, doing chores at home, and so on. Develop their emotional, mental and physical stamina so that they can handle what comes their way in life without falling apart.

16. Embrace Imperfections

We are all human beings with imperfections. Your child has their imperfections as well. Do not expect more from your child than they can give. It is true every parent's goal is to see their child succeed and do the right thing, but helping them succeed does not mean they cannot make mistakes. Leave room for shortcomings. Not everything your child does wrong should be an issue for you. Let go of some things; pick your battles wisely. Understand that you have your own imperfections as well. It is our imperfections that make us complete human beings. As you lead your child to do what is right, ignore things that are not life-threatening. Think about some imperfections that you can easily overlook. For example, if your child makes a mess on a clean carpet, you can overlook it because it is not a major harm. Clean it up, and move on with life. Let go of battles that are not worth the fight.

17. Focus on Strengths

Find the good in your child and in everything they do. Find the good in their intentions. Many parents tend to look for what is wrong – the bad things – but many children are not intentionally bad. In their minds, they are doing their best and giving their best. Look for areas of strength, not weakness. What are your child's strengths? Take a minute to think about that, and write it down. When you identify and know your child's strengths, you will tend to work from within those parameters. You will be more forgiving of their weaknesses and imperfections. When you know their strengths, share it with them; this will boost their confidence to know that they have strengths in certain things. Always highlight your child's strengths to them and encourage them to focus on doing more of what they love and know to do well.

18. Express Appreciation

There is a lot to be thankful for in your life. Even when you think and feel everything is falling apart, behind the clouds is a rainbow. Behind every difficult situation is a silver lining. You can always find something good in every situation which you can be grateful and express appreciation for. Express appreciation for the fact that you are alive and have the opportunity to turn any circumstance around. Express appreciation for your children. Express appreciation for the sun that shines giving you hope for a new day. When you express appreciation for what is, the universe will conspire to give you more. If you are sad and downtrodden and see the bad in every circumstance, you will draw more negativity towards you. Always look for the good in every situation and have an aura of gratitude about you. If your child makes a mistake, forgive them and be grateful for your child. Let go of things that do not serve you positively, and express appreciation for what is and what could be.

19. Lead by Example

As a parent, you are also a leader. You are in a position to lead your child to be an accomplished, successful, grounded and whole person who will positively impact the world around them. This means that you have to be the right kind of leader. You have to lead by example. You have to exhibit habits that are worth emulating. You do not only lead by words; you lead by actions as well. Honor your word, and let your actions speak for you. Do what you say you will do. Are you telling your child not to do something but you are doing it yourself? You cannot expect from others what you cannot give. That is hypocritical. Be exemplary in your behaviors so that even without saying a word, your child can look up to you as their role model – someone they are inspired by and would like to be like.

20. Celebrate Achievements

Never take your child's accomplishments for granted. Make a big deal about the little, amazing things they do every day, including their achievements at school. If your child moves their grades from a D to a C, celebrate that. If your child spends extra time studying or reading, express your pride in them. If your child performs a random act of kindness and does something nice for someone else, celebrate them. Celebrating achievements does not mean going overboard or throwing a big party. Something as simple as buying them ice cream, or their favorite snack, or giving them a big high-five and a big hug is enough. The main thing is for them to see you recognize what they have done and that you are proud of them for making the effort to accomplish it.

21. Know Your Rights

As a parent, you have many rights. Some of your rights include providing educational access and resources for your child. Be sure to uphold your rights in your child's best interest. Some of those include the availability of resources that your child can benefit from to enhance their education. Look in the parent handbook of your child's school, or inquire with your local district or head office. Knowing your rights does not mean irrationally demanding and enforcing them. Understand that the school has your child's best interest at heart. Most administrators want their students to succeed, so barring errors and compliance issues, schools have good faith in ensuring that your child succeeds. Keep this in the back of your mind while objectively enforcing your rights as a parent.

22. Be Disciplined

Discipline is key in raising children. You have to be disciplined to raise a disciplined person. You have to discipline your child, and you have to have disciplined habits that provide structure and consistency for your child. Personal discipline means maintaining order and structure in your life. It means running a home environment that is focused, structured and organized. People who are disciplined get things done. They know what needs to be done, and they avoid all distractions and obstacles that prevent them from doing it. Parents who are not disciplined lack consistency. They are not focused. They are very sporadic and often spontaneous in their actions. Lack of consistency can adversely impact your child because they are not sure what to expect from you from one moment to the next. When you are disciplined, you teach your child to be disciplined as well. Your child needs discipline to get their school work done.

23. Be Consistent

Consistency shows discipline. It shows that you follow through and do the things you say you will do. It shows you are grounded. When a parent is consistent, it is great for their child because their child knows what to expect from them. For children, consistency means safety, security, and predictability. Consistency gives them the comfort of knowing what to expect from you as their parent. Parents who are not consistent rattle their children, because they doubt what their parent will do next. They become unsure of themselves, as well. It leaves them wondering what will happen next. Be consistent in your day-to-day life as a parent and as a person. Establish some basic rules and routines at home, make them known to your child, and consistently apply them so your child knows what to expect. Have some values that you consistently apply in your life. Doing so makes your life more predictable and less erratic.

24. Focus on Yourself

Social media has truly transformed the way people live their lives. So much of people's personal lives is being exposed to the public. This exposure is a reflection of free speech and free expression. The danger in this is it forces people to try to mirror the lifestyle and values of others. It causes individuals to measure their lives in unrealistic ways. Focus on yourself and your family. Take some time to think about your family values – the principles and morals that govern your family. Focus on the things that matter to you. Focus on your circumstances and reality. Never try to measure yourself against someone else, because there is always more to their story than you see. Live life within your means, based on what you can afford. Stop comparing yourself to others.

25. No Excuses

Money is tight for many families today. Your family may be one of those feeling the financial pinch. Do not let money interfere with your desire to help your child succeed. I once heard the story of two Mexican immigrants who had no money at all. They made a living in the dark streets of Los Angeles recycling trash for cash. When their oldest son was failing in school, they took him to the streets of Los Angeles at night and made him pick bottles with them to picture a future without an education. The child moved his grades up and received scholarships to pursue a degree in aerospace engineering at the Michigan Institute of Technology. This family did not have money, but they did have a vision for their child. So let your principles about a good education drive you, not your money situation. Do not make excuses that compromise your child's future.

26. Believe in Your Child

Even if the story of the bumblebee is a fable, the moral of the story teaches a powerful lesson. The story is that scientists said the bumblebee would never fly because its wings are too narrow to carry its large, heavy body. But one day the bumblebee got up and flew. One observer noted the bumblebee flew because no one had told the bumblebee it could not fly. The moral here is "believe in your child." They are born with gifts and talents; the words, tone of voice, and actions you use daily can either nurture or downplay that talent. Like the bumblebee, every single child can use their skills to succeed. When you encourage and nurture the gifts within your child, they will grow up to harness the power that lies within them.

27. Give Direction

Children need the direction of their parents. While this is a true statement, there are times when children themselves will resist the direction of their parents. As a parent, it is your responsibility to help your child see future possibilities, and what actions and behaviors they need to adopt now to put them on course for great things in life. Talk to your child about the various options and paths that can help them further their success. Talk to them about staying on course and staying focused, about having a sense of direction that leads them to reach the goals they have for their lives. Parents who do not give their children direction fail to secure a future for them because the children are left with no sense of purpose. Talk to your child about why they go to school, about why it is important to do well in school.

28. Teach Contentment

Contentment is not an often-used word, but it is one which can make a powerful difference in your child's life. We are all familiar with how peer pressure impacts so many children. The need to fit in and be accepted by peers is important to some students. But if your child is content with themselves, this need dissipates. Teach your child contentment; to be happy with who they are and what they have. Teach your child to realize that within them lies the power to create their own reality, their own life, without being influenced by others. Teach them that although they may not have what others have, what they do have is sufficient to impact their own reality. When your child is content with their life, they will have less emotional, mental and psychological problems in the future. They will learn to avoid measuring themselves against others.

29. Safety First

I had a phone conversation with a friend the other day, and we shared our fears about being parents in the world today. There is just so much bad news out there, which seems to spread faster than the good news. As I watch the world become a more violent and intolerant place, I realize there's no better time than now to hug your child and teach them love, peace, empathy, and understanding. Also, ensure that you maintain your role as a provider and safety net for your child. Avoid decisions and choices that put your child in harm's way. Watch out for people – strangers – you bring around your child. Not all of them have the best interests of you or your child at heart. They may just be a snake waiting to unleash their venom. It is better to err for your child's safety. Dedicate your time to making sure that your child is safe. Keep your eyes on them at all times.

30. Create a New Reality

One of the most powerful lessons I have learned in life is that one's situation is not final. There is always a solution to every problem. No matter what you may be faced with in life, you can always make choices which will help you create a new reality. So, if there is something in your family life that you do not like, create a new reality. If you are having problems in your relationship and do not like how you are being treated, create a new reality. If you have a child who is defiant or struggling in school, create a new reality. Find out what are the things that bother you about your current situation, then ask yourself specifically what you can do to turn things around and create a new reality for yourself and your family. There is no reason to wallow in a situation for too long, or let it get you down. You have a choice. Think clearly about how you can change the situation.

31. Monitor TV

Several studies have shown the impact that TV watching has on productivity, for both adults and children. Education statistics have shown that too much TV affects a child's performance in school, in general, and math in particular. For some parents, it is tempting just to let their children watch TV, to get them distracted or to keep them busy. Smart parenting, however, requires you to think of the consequences of doing this on a consistent basis. Too much TV prevents children from doing other more productive activities, like reading, focusing on effectively completing their homework, cleaning their room, staying organized, and so on. Even worse, TV causes many children to have attention problems. So monitor your child's use of Television. Make sure they use it after they have done their homework. Also, limit the amount of time they use it.

32. Monitor Devices

Advances in technology have made life a little more sophisticated in how we access information. There are so many mediums by which we can view information visually. There is a whole range of screens – such as laptops, tablets, phones, and a variety of other hand-held devices – that are easily accessible. Increasingly, a lot of parents are making these devices available to their children, some to make information accessible to them and others just because they want their children to have them. It is important to remember that these devices can achieve the opposite effect of what you want them to do if they are not closely monitored. Teach your child how to effectively use the devices in a way that works to their advantage and does not distract them. They can use them for school research, to gain some new ideas, or in other ways that advance their interest in very real ways. Teach them the impact that constantly staring at these devices have on them, visually and regarding their productivity.

33. Mindset Trumps Language Barrier

I have had the privilege of working with several second-language learners during my years as a teacher. I have seen, first-hand, the impact that language has on student learning, especially in English language arts. I have also seen many families – parents and children – defy language barriers and achieve success. In these cases, parents made success and learning non-negotiable. They encouraged their children to focus in school, develop a learning mindset, and break language barriers to access information. When the home environment is conducive to learning, and when parents instill the mindset that success is the end-goal, children naturally develop the fortitude to make it true. When you implement the right systems, values, mindset, structure, and environment at home, you help your child nurture the skills and habits that make success inevitable, despite any language barrier.

34. Your Values

Who are you? What do you stand for? What do you believe about world peace? What do you believe about forgiveness? What do you believe about relationships? What do you believe about living meaningfully? These questions are at the core of the values, principles, and beliefs which drive your everyday life. So many adults and children struggle to find themselves in this ever-changing world because they have no values. It is so essential to have sound values and principles which define your children, give them a strong sense of self, and help them find inner peace. I see many children who are confused about their identity; when I look at their parents, I see that they, too, are confused about their identity. Teach your child that they are beautiful, they are strong, and they have something valuable to give to the world.

35. Money-Wise

In the majority of cases, children learn money-saving habits from their parents. Children also learn to spend money the way their parents spend money. If you are an extravagant parent who spends money at will, your child will likely spend money at will as well. If you are a parent who is more frugal, loves to save, or shows that money has value and should be reasonably spent, your child will likely reflect those money values as well. Many schools do not teach financial literacy, so your child will more than likely learn their money habits from you. Be aware of what kind of money values you instill in your child. These values vary from family to family, based on their income reality, so no one money principle fits all families. However, be deliberate in how and what you teach your child about saving, investing, budgeting and donating money.

36. Have a Vision

Many people say that as parents, you cannot tell your child what to do in life or what career to pursue. You cannot design their future for them. You have to let them choose their life path and make decisions for themselves. When you force your child into a certain corner, it may not be the right fit based on who they are and their personal preferences. However, it is essential to have a vision for your child, a vision that lets you see their future and shows you the kind of life and lifestyle you would like them to have. This vision must be crystal clear to you. It is that vision which will define your actions today. What vision do you have for your child? What can you do today to ensure that they live the life you dream about for them? If your vision is to see your child able to care for themselves financially, then work today to create that reality.

37. Never Quit on Yourself

Many parents experience uphill battles in life. At some point in every human being's life, there will be temptations, trials, and tribulations. There will be hardships that will cause you to reach your brink. If you ever get to this point, and I hope you never do, I want to encourage you to hold on through your struggle and pain. Grow a backbone and stand your ground. Never let your circumstances overwhelm you. Have a mindset of giving your child the best in every circumstance, or teach them how to cope with every situation. Ironically, no matter what we may be going through in our personal lives, we still have to stand tall – for our children. You cannot fall apart, because your child will fall apart, too. So in the midst of all the challenges you may be experiencing, do not just survive, thrive. Come out of it all standing tall.

38. Pray

Prayer is powerful. Prayers avail much. Talking to God about your problems and asking Him to intervene to solve your problems is one of the most powerful actions you can take to help you get out of any situation. Make it a habit to pray daily. Pray for your child and with your child. Pray about any situation. God is a God of abundance; He created the whole universe. If He can do that, He can solve your problem. But you have to have faith and trust that God will do it. If your children are acting out, misbehaving, not doing well in school, or not being obedient, form a family circle by holding their hands and pray. In the privacy of your room, pray to God and ask Him to give you wisdom, direction, understanding, and discernment. Ask Him to directly handle the problem from Heaven. There are many miracles that only He can handle, and He does every single time.

39. Decide on a Major

I encourage both you and your child to do some in-depth research online to help your child find a college major that aligns with their passions, skills, talents, future goals, and dreams. When you do your due diligence, and come up with a major, encourage your child to stick with this major through college; switching majors can be very costly, in terms of time and money. If a student is consistent and sticks to a major with a good job prospect or career outlook, they can start earning a good salary by the age of 30. Have this conversation with your child; talk to them about why staying consistent in their major will get them out of school faster, and start earning an income sooner. Discourage them from switching between courses and not achieving anything of substance. Students who are undecided about what major to pursue stay in school much longer.

40. Save for College

Money is tight for many families. Most people are just getting by and have just enough to spend on living expenses. For struggling families, saving for college is simply out of the question; there is nothing extra to put aside. Where will it come from? While this is often true, I also believe that living without any savings is the riskiest thing to do in life. You have to put money aside for rainy days and your children's education; it is an investment in a successful future. If you save and send your child to college, you are ensuring they get a good job, and this brings a return on your investment. So where do you find that extra money? Cut back on your expenses – cable, utilities, eating out – get a second job, save!

41. Speak Up

Many children are afraid to speak up. They are intimidated to share their opinion in public, especially when adults are present. Where does this fear come from? It is fear of being criticized, appearing stupid, or not making sense; it is fear that your point is not worth its weight. It is widely said the fear of public speaking is the biggest fear most people have. It speaks to our belief systems. Encourage your child to develop a belief in self, to speak up when they have something to say, and never be afraid to share what they know. Encourage them to trust their judgment and to trust themselves. It is something you have to consistently do to help your child grow. Give them opportunities to speak up, such as reading announcements in church or doing skits and performances in front of the family. Teach them to speak up.

42. The Path of Least Resistance

Life is so comfortable for some children; they do not want to be bothered with going the extra mile. Part of the reason is their parents have provided everything for them, and there is nothing more they need. The other aspect is a lack of motivation to pursue bigger goals and reach for more. Therefore, they settle. They settle for what *is*. They settle for *less*. They settle for *comfortable*. They choose the path of least resistance. When you help your child realize that they have a giant inside of them, that they can do anything they set their mind to, you will begin to help them take brave and bold steps to make bigger things happen in their life. Teach them that life is hard, but if they are willing to go through the tough times, they will come out victorious.

43. The Right Major

The right major in school makes a huge difference in a child's future lifestyle. Income-wise, certain majors make more sense than others. A degree in Biochemistry will earn more money than a degree in Anthropology. Encourage your child to choose a major that makes sense financially and will be worth the cost of paying college costs. For many families who do not have enough money, the right major will help their children earn enough to cover their living expenses. It is true that money is not the only factor in pursuing a major, but money is certainly important in helping a person pay their bills and expenses. Encourage your child to do their research and pursue a career that will help them be comfortable in life and not have to struggle for money. The standard of living is getting higher, so get your child ready.

44. Unique and Original

When a newborn comes into the world, you can never find anything wrong with them. Even if they are born with known and visible disabilities, everyone looks at babies as fully possessing beautiful qualities. They are precious, amazing and awesome. They are free of worldly influence, and we look at them as adorable and possessing all they need to excel in life. Unfortunately, something happens to children along the way. They start getting influenced by the world, and by those around them. But if you see your child the way they were born – fearfully and wonderfully made – you will realize that they have the power to achieve impossible things. Teach them to see themselves as someone with incredible personal power. Teach them to develop the mindset and have the courage to tap their personal power to reach their goals. When a child believes that they are unique and truly capable, their self-belief grows, and they achieve more.

45. One-on-One Time

Time is one of the most precious gifts today. We live in a rat race; life is so fast-paced; parents are busy, children are busy. There is just so much to accomplish in one day. Life has to go on because families need to do what they need to do to survive in a money-driven economy. In the midst of your busy schedule, find a way to create one-on-one time with your children; this is so critical in helping them develop into the person you want them to be. They need the comfort and assurance of your love and your presence. If you are too busy and cannot spend time with them, let them know and ask them to support you as you do what needs to be done to provide for their needs. Use every free moment you have to bond and spend time with them because life moves too fast. If you cannot see them for long periods of time, check in with them throughout the day by text message to see how they are doing.

46. Undivided Attention

Your undivided attention makes your child feel heard and valued. It is important to give your child undivided attention when they have something to say to you. If you are reading a book, working on the computer, or doing something else, and your child needs to talk to you, take the time to stop what you are doing, look at them, and listen to what they have to say. You no doubt have a very busy schedule, but whenever your time frees up spend it with your child. Enjoy their company, talk with them about life, about what is important to them and you. I believe when we have children, life comes down to the moments we spend with them. Children also love to be in the company of their parents. They love it when their parents make them feel valued and that they matter; this boosts their self-esteem.

47. Declare Greatness

Believe and declare that your child has greatness within them. Never stop telling them that they have the power to design and create the life of their dreams. Raise your child in such a way that they will have the courage to speak up, the courage to be bold. Teach them to realize the power that lies within them; the power to believe in who they are, to trust themselves more. The power to recognize their talent and work to enhance their talents for their good. The power to resist peer pressure and any form of intimidation. When your child recognizes their greatness and power, they will make decisions that will change their life for good. They will make decisions that reflect their self-belief. They will trust themselves to know that their life is in their hands, and they can achieve their goals and dreams.

48. Teach Responsibility

Every parent's wish is to ensure that their child does not struggle. Their goal is to see their child happy, healthy and in no kind of pain, struggle, or lack. Some parents do not assign their children chores at home because they think it will strain their child. While we want our children to be happy and healthy, you have to let them do some heavy lifting themselves. Not only does this teach them responsibility, but it also helps them develop grit, stamina, and resilience to face and surmount obstacles. You can help your child by letting them do some work, to face a little resistance. Let them do chores at home – wash the dishes, do laundry, clean the house, cook, take out the trash, run errands, and whatever else needs to be done. You are not punishing them by making them do this. They are doing work that will make them stronger and prepare them to effectively run their life.

49. Bond

Your lovely, amazing child lives in a world that is fast-changing and ever so busy. Distractions have reached new heights. How will you, as a parent, help your child find themselves in the maze of all that is happening around them? How will you help them discover who they truly are, and avoid being vulnerable to other people's values, opinions, decisions, and choices? How will you help your child to be themselves in a world of copycats? In a world where everyone is trying to fit in? How will you help your child discover their identity and uniqueness? I will tell you: by bonding with them. Having a close enough relationship where they value you and feel accepted and loved in their home environment. Re-evaluate and create ways to share more intimate moments to nurture who they are and help them feel great about themselves. Use every opportunity for bonding with your child, instead of browsing the Internet!

50. A Gem

A gem is something that is absolutely great! Something that is amazingly beautiful and almost perfect, if not perfect. When most people think of a gem, they usually think of precious jewelry, like gold, diamonds or rhinestones. Those who possess a gem treat it with extreme care. They place it in a specific place, take of it, and ensure it is safe, and nobody comes close to it. Do you think your child is a gem? Do you think they are precious and rare? If you do, then you will treat them as such. You will invest all your energies to ensure that they are taken care of. You will watch the words you use to speak to them and around them. You will be more careful how you respond to their needs. You will be more careful in ensuring their safety. Remember: you only have one gem, one child. They are unique and special, and you must give them your best to ensure they are whole and grounded.

51. No Comparison

Contentment is the willingness to live with who you are and what you have; to accept your life the way it is and seek to make meaningful change only in the direction that you think is best for your circumstances. Never envy or seek to be like someone else. Never envy another's life because you do not know their battles, their struggles, or their reality. Take stock of your situation, and if there is something you'd like to change about yourself, put yourself in the position to work on it – but do it for you, not to impress others. Be assured, when God created you and your children, He made you complete in His image. He created in you the spirit and heart to live your life fully with what He gave you. He gave you the ability and talents to foster your future. Use them for your good! Do not compare yourself with others.

52. Circumstances

I always share the story of my life growing up as a little girl in Africa. I grew up in a culture where little girls were stereotyped to specific roles and social expectations. For instance, many girls cannot sit amongst house guests, share their thoughts in front of adults, or be overambitious in seeking success for themselves. Your duty, as a girl, is to cook, clean, take care of others, and act a certain way. So I grew up in a box. I grew up knowing there were certain boundaries I could not cross. Despite all that, I believed in my strength and abilities. I knew I had inherent gifts and talents but needed the right environment to nurture and express them. If you live in an environment which stifles your growth, remember that you have gifts and talents. Always look for opportunities to nurture and unleash your talents. Never let what is happening in your environment impede your progress. Never let your circumstances limit you!

53. Seize Opportunities

You have heard this enough, and it is worth repeating: America is the land of opportunity. Opportunities abound in America. They are everywhere. When I was in Cameroon, I sent out many letters applying for scholarships. I received one positive response that changed my life forever. My story could be your child's story. Encourage your child to seek and apply for opportunities that will help them move their life forward. There are a ton of free resources and free funds available that can help your child reach their academic goals. Do a Google search for those opportunities, or visit my website at www.nicolineambe.com/scholarships. Visit the link and take time out of your day to apply for as many of these as possible. It is especially important to seek these free resources if you have limited income. All you need to do is allocate time to do this.

54. Talk About School

Develop your child's interest in learning by consistently talking to them about school. Find out what happens in school on a daily basis. Find out about their classes. Ask them to share stories about their teachers and other students. Find out what incidences occurred in school. Find out what they think about their courses and the instructors. Find out how they can adjust and improve their learning habits to grow academically. Talk to them about how education translates to a successful future, and why the journey is worth it. Help your child develop a learning mindset by having consistent and thoughtful conversations with them about the value and benefit of school. Also, share your expectations with them, and discuss what kind of results will help them improve their life choices as adults. When you share your expectations, children usually rise to meet them.

55. Encourage Reading

You have heard of the saying, "readers are leaders." One of the most interesting things I have read is that the most successful people in the world are those who continue to be voracious readers. Why do they even bother to read when they are already so successful? Reading is precisely *why* they are successful; because when you read, you open your mind to new possibilities. You expand your thinking. To know more, you have to read more. Reading helps you develop your ideas. It helps you increase your knowledge of what you already know. When students read, they increase their understanding of the content. They expose themselves to new information. They learn a great deal. So encourage your child to be a voracious reader. Encourage them to read books on subjects that are of interest to them. Encourage them to read for an additional 30 minutes after completing their homework. Readers are achievers!

56. A Learning Environment

Your home environment should reflect a place of learning – if not physically, then psychologically. As much as possible, have books available for your child to read. You can borrow books from the library, or borrow them from your child's teacher. Have magazines at home for your child to browse. If you do not have any of these things, you can still create a learning environment by turning off the TV, video games, and gadgets, and encourage your child to just go over their school work. Also, let your child see you take reading seriously. Let your child observe you working on things, on your own goals, on your own projects, and getting things done. A learning environment does not necessarily mean the presence of books in the home. It could just be the aura you give off as a parent about the importance of reading and learning and the outcome they produce.

57. Talk to the Teacher

One thing I know about teachers: they love to help! They love to see their students do well. Not only is it good for the student, but it also makes the teacher look good. It means the student has learned something from their teaching and instruction. Based on that, teachers are willing to intervene and help any student who is struggling, or who needs additional support in reaching their academic milestones. If you have any questions or concerns about how your child is performing in school, never hesitate to talk to their teacher. Talk to them about anything. Ask their opinion on anything. Ask them what additional resources are available that can help your child succeed. Ask them to provide you with free books that your child can read at home. If you are concerned about your child's performance, ask them what you can do at home to help your child excel.

58. Limit Screen Exposure

Several statistics document the impact that TV and video games have on children, especially children with attention problems. TV is distracting, even for adults. If used mindlessly, TV and video games can prevent children from getting their work done. Not only will it steal their time, but it will also keep them from focusing on the assignment itself. These forms of technology rattle children's brains and increase their brain activity. So as much as possible, limit them to ensure that they are used wisely. Limit your child to specific times when they can use these devices and times when they need to be completing their homework. After they have finished their homework, they can use these devices as a break from school work. TV can sometimes be a great idea if used for educational purposes, and children who are visual learners. So be sure that the TV program is enriching.

59. Stay Organized

Organization is key to getting things done. When someone is organized in their physical world, they will also be organized in their thinking. They will get things done. Help your child stay organized, to keep track of paperwork, to keep track of their assignments and homework, and to keep their environment orderly. One of the best ways of staying organized is to have a calendar where things can be written down. Get one with large boxes so there is room to write, and keep it in a central location in your home where you and your child will see it. Some children can even use their phones to log in details. Encourage your child to keep a daily to-do list, to write down the things they need to accomplish for the day, and to write down when assignments are due; this is the most powerful way to ensure things get done. Your child can check items off the list as they are completed.

60. Reading Skills

Effective reading skills are an important part of success. Honing good reading skills is essential to help children improve fluency and comprehension. Have your child study the book cover and ask themselves what information is presented on the front and back cover of the book which will help them predict what will be in the text? Sometimes, it will take more than one or two reads to fully understand the context and content of the reading. Teach your child to be patient and go over the information as many times as they need to learn it. Encourage your child to take notes as they read, identify the main points, use flash cards and highlighters to highlight major points. Encourage them to scan the chapters, and also use diagrams and thinking maps to organize their ideas.

61. Engage in Class

Engagement is one of the main keys to academic success. Encourage your child to listen to their teacher, to pay close attention to everything that the teacher is saying in class. Most of what will be on the test, quiz, or homework will be taught in class. Unless your child reads the class materials on their own, the only other way of knowing the information is by listening and paying close attention in class. Encourage them to stay focused in class, and to take good notes whenever possible. Encourage them to stay engaged in classroom discussions; to participate and raise their hands to answer questions; to avoid distractions by other students; to contribute to group discussions and projects. Encourage your child to ask for clarification if there is something they do not quite understand – but they have to be engaged to know what to ask.

62. Homework

Homework counts for a large part of your child's grade. Encourage your child to complete and turn in every single homework assignment that is due. Also, make sure they *know* exactly what the teacher is asking for in the homework, and *do* exactly what the teacher is asking for in the homework. You do not need to help your child with their homework. If you must assist them, make sure you do not confuse them with techniques they may not have learned in class. A lot of children resist homework help from their parents because their parents do not teach it the same way the teacher taught; this frustrates them. Your main responsibility as far as homework is concerned, is to provide a quiet environment at home where your child can complete their homework without disruptions and noise. Then monitor them and praise them for their effort.

63. Provide a Balanced Life

Help your child develop balance in their life. Help them understand the various components in their life and work to satisfy all. Our lives are made up of our work, our health, our relationships (social) and our spiritual life. All of these components are essential to make life more beautiful. You cannot work to the detriment of your health. You cannot forgo or abandon your personal relationships because of work. Children tend to focus more on the social aspects of their relationships, but you have to stress to them the importance of all aspects. Live your life to reflect this truth and your child will follow your example. Provide balance in your child's life by raising them to experience various aspects of life. As your child grows up, they will begin to appreciate the beauty of life and live more fully.

64. Relate With the Teacher

Study your child's work carefully to ensure they are not falling behind in classwork, and to make sure they are on top of the content. When you see your child struggling or needing more help, be sure to contact the teacher or encourage your child to talk to their teacher. It is essential that you have a good relationship with your child's teacher, especially if your child is experiencing difficulties. If you do not have a good relationship with your child's teacher, then you will not be able to communicate your needs. Unfortunately, some parents like to argue; they pick fights with the teacher and always take their child's side, even when they should be more objective; this is not smart. Most teachers are very reasonable and want their students to succeed. Have an open and mutual relationship that allows you to communicate your needs with them. Encourage your child to do the same. Teachers are very receptive to students and parents who show an interest in academic success.

65. Listen Carefully

Listening is one of the most powerful aspects of any relationship, but it is also one of the most overlooked. Make an effort to listen to your child. People feel valued when they are listened to – when they feel heard – especially children. It is emotionally satisfying. It means their point of view counts. It means *who they are* counts. It means you value them and hold them in high esteem. Never take listening for granted. If your child is saying something to you, make it a point to stop what you are doing and listen. Answer their questions and ensure they are satisfied with your response. If what they are saying does not make sense to you, ask them to repeat what they said so you could offer a response. Many times, children just want to feel heard. Ask questions if you have to, because it shows you are listening.

66. A Warm Home

A warm and caring home is essential to your child's success in school and in life. It is essential to their sense of well-being and feeling of safety. A warm and caring home tells children that they have a place where they can be who they want to be, where they are not judged for their flaws. A place where they can freely express themselves without fear of repercussion. A place that is predictable. A place where there is no screaming, no loud arguing between spouses and children. A place where children have something to eat after a long day at school. A place where they can enjoy quiet while doing their homework. A place where people genuinely care for one another and look out for each other. A place where children can count on their parents and parents can count on their children to each do their part. A place of love. A place to come to for peace, after a long day in the wild world.

67. Love Your Child

Love your child unconditionally, with everything that is in you. Live daily in the awareness that your primary job as a parent is to fulfill your child's emotional and physical needs and ensure that they become a well-rounded, happy, and productive human being. Know that an essential part of helping your child achieve this is showing them love – love in how you communicate, how you relate to them, how you handle their mistakes, how you respond when they frustrate you. Love is calm, love is energy, love is patient. Put love at the forefront of your parental decisions. When your child feels loved, they enjoy inner peace, experience calm, and feel a sense of assurance that radiates to other aspects of their life. Love your child intentionally and consciously, knowing that this will make a difference in how they relate to the world around them.

68. Words Have Power

The words that come out of your mouth hold such significance in the grand scheme of your child's life. Many parents underestimate the power of their words on their children's feelings, and ultimately in their lives. Do not use discouraging words around your children, because words have power. Use words of encouragement which make them feel they can achieve anything, and that they can be successful. Never put your children down or make them feel inadequate. Always boost their self-confidence with encouraging words. It is natural for parents to scold their children, and sometimes many have to raise their voices in doing so. That is normal, but discipline your children with love. Use words which make them understand that even though you are scolding them, you still love them, and you are looking out for their best interest.

69. Failure Is Not an Option

When you raise your children to have a winning mindset, you give them a proper perspective to deal with failure. You help them see failure for what it is – an acceptable part of the process. It is acceptable to experience temporary failures and setbacks. That is a fundamental part of the process of growing up. Teach your children that failure is not an option as an outcome, and that they must always get back up and give it their best one more time, each and every time. Do not raise a quitter – a child who says "I can't do it." Raise your expectations so that your child understands that you do not accept poor performance from them. Help your children develop a work ethic that encourages them to want to give their best in everything they do; to put in their best work, and make no compromises as far as their academic performance is concerned; to know what to adjust when they make a mistake, and to adjust every time they make a mistake. The bottom line is to raise your child never to give up, and to always want to be better.

70. Mental Discipline

One of the most efficient ways to assist your child with homework is to provide a quiet, structured environment where they can focus and figure out the information *by themselves*. Encourage your child to think and reason through the problem. A quiet home environment helps children to pay more attention and persevere, even with difficult tasks. It is important for children to build their focus and independent thinking skills because these will become crucial in higher grades when the curriculum is more challenging. Encourage your child to rely on their mental resources. That way, even if you cannot help due to the complexity of the content, your child will have developed the skills necessary to complete their work independently.

71. A Quiet Study Area

Your child's study environment is paramount to their success in school. So be intentional about providing your child with an environment that makes learning easy. Provide your child with a quiet study environment with adequate lighting and a desk or writing surface. If possible, make it an exclusive study area for your child. Eliminate distractions such as Television, stereo, telephone, and so on; this will help them discern challenging content by allowing them to focus and concentrate. Good study habits are extremely crucial for children to develop at a very early age. These habits will not only help them through school, but they will also assist them in developing the discipline to work efficiently in their future professional working world. Think about your child's study area now. Is it quiet? Do they have a space of their own? If not, be sure to provide these.

72. A Good Night's Sleep

Ensure that your child has a good night's sleep daily. Consistent, strict, and early bedtimes help children to be more alert and focus in class. Students can discern difficult comprehension, literacy, and math tasks when they have had sufficient rest. Students who have set early bedtimes out-perform their sleep-deprived counterparts. They are sharper in class, think through questions faster, and are more accurate in their analysis of the issues. Several scientific studies show that children need nine to ten hours of sleep and that regular and consistent bedtime helps with brain development. Creating a bedtime routine also teaches your child to be responsible, and value time. Have your children set their alarm clock and wake themselves in the morning. Not only does this teach them to be independent, but it also takes away some responsibility from you and makes morning routines a little easier.

73. Show Interest in School

Show your child that you are interested in school. Place a value on school and present it as the only option in your home. Make school a non-negotiable goal for your children. Always speak about what school will do for them, how it will help them do well in life. Create an environment at home that is consistent with your beliefs and values about school. Create a routine that lets your children know you are interested in their school work. Check in with your child consistently to ask how they are doing in school and discuss their experiences. Ask about their day and show interest in the stories and experiences they share with you about school. Ask about their friends and their group projects. Provide your children all the school supplies they need to complete their projects and assignments.

74. Respect for Others

Encourage your children to have respect for others, and to show simple courtesies in social settings. Many children these days will walk past you, or bump into you, and not say excuse me. They do not have the courtesy to wait and be patient, to give someone else the opportunity to go ahead. Teach your children to say please and thank you. Teach your children to refer to people by their titles, to be respectful to leaders and those older than them. Teach them to empathize with the pain and sufferings of others; to put themselves in other people's shoes; to value relationships over material things. Helping your children be respectful entails spending time with them and talking to them about life and about what is appropriate. If you are a Christian, take your child to church and help them develop a spirit of caring and love for others.

75. Responsible Behavior

As a parent, when you successfully help your child take responsibility for their actions you take some of the workload off your shoulders and, at the same time, help your child to become more independent. Teach your child to see the impact of their actions by looking at how those actions affect their life, and the lives of others, either positively or negatively. Taking responsibility for one's actions means doing the things you need to do when you ought to do them. It means not making excuses about how you cannot do things you are supposed to be doing. Think about it. What kind of things do you hold your child responsible for? What would you like to see them take responsibility for? Be sure to express that to them in specific ways. Sometimes, children are not aware because a parent has not taken the time to talk to them. When people know better, they do better. So tell your children what you expect of them.

76. Health Check-ups

Your child's health has a direct correlation to their school work. Be sure to feed your child healthy fruits and vegetables daily. Studies show that brain function improves tremendously in children who eat healthy, nutritious meals daily. Also, take your child in for regular dental check-ups every six months or yearly. Tooth decay has become a serious crisis with many children who load up on sugar daily. In the long run, this will lead to overall health issues that could lead to heart disease, high blood pressure, and even diabetes. Make sure your child brushes their teeth twice daily at least. Overall health is key to effective brain function; by helping your child develop these healthy habits early on, you will help them be well on their way to overall excellence in body, mind, and spirit. You also have to lead by example by doing these things for yourself – staying healthy and having regular doctor and dental checkups.

77. A Good Education

As a parent, you have to be positive about how a good education will benefit your child. Do not do and say things to discourage your child about the importance of school. You have to consistently stress the value of a good education, and help your child see why school is an important part of their lives now and in the future. Part of doing this is ensuring you create an environment at home which is conducive to learning, an environment which is quiet and lets your child know what they should be doing at home and what their priority should be at any given time. As an educator, I see many parents who struggle to implement simple rules and expectations that enhance their children's educational priority. They do not stress reading, studying, and efficient work habits in their children. As a result, their children do not think it is important to take their education seriously. These are the students who consistently fail to meet grade-level standards.

78. Be Positive About Math

Math is one of those subjects that unnecessarily scares many people. Many students feel apprehensive about their math class because they have not been adequately coached and mentored on how to properly study the subject. As a parent, it is important to set your child on a firm foundation when it comes to learning math. Let go of your apprehensions about the subject. Make sure that from a very early grade, your child understands their math facts and basic math concepts like addition, subtraction, multiplication, and division. All other math concepts in later grades are built on these early fundamentals. Track your child's performance in math by looking at their homework assignments, test scores, and work samples to ensure they are scoring high. If you see any problems, intervene immediately. In the current job market, math and other subjects in the STEM field are ear-marked for getting good jobs and scholarships for college.

79. Back-to-School Night

Back-to-school night sets the stage for a successful and focused school year. It creates the right academic mood for your child as the year kicks off. Be sure to attend each one, every year, to learn about your child's teachers. Talk to them about your child, even pick a seat for your child. Learn about the course load and workload, find out about assignments, grading and grade level expectations, ask the teacher questions to gain clarity on things you do not fully understand. Take your child with you for back-to-school night, and talk to them about your expectations for school success, based on the information you receive from back-to-school night. You prepare your child for a successful school year by knowing what is ahead. Be an involved and informed parent because this shows your child how much you value education.

80. Parent-Teacher Meetings

Parent-teacher meetings give you direct information about your child's performance and achievement. To provide support and direction for your child, you have to know exactly where they are in their school work. Before attending the meeting with your child's teacher, make a list of all the things you need to ask. What questions are on your mind? What concerns you about your child's education? What do you have doubts about? What would you like to discuss more? Be sure to ask every question. Find out what you can do at home to help your child improve their academic performance. Find out what resources are available at school for your child. To have an effective parent-teacher meeting, you must be aware of how your child is performing in school. Once you have this information, you can ask the right questions.

81. Volunteer at School

Parents choose to volunteer at their children's schools for many different reasons. Some do it because they love the school and want to give back; for others, it is mandatory, especially in some private schools; and others do it to provide supervision for their children. Some students, especially when they are much younger, work better when a parent is present in the classroom. Teachers appreciate parent volunteers because of the added help they provide. Volunteering also enhances the community spirit of the school; it is an excellent example of the quote, *"it takes a village to raise a child."* A little goes a long way. If you have the time, spend once a week or once a month helping out at your child's school. Make copies, distribute flyers, organize a fundraiser, send out emails, or doing whatever needs to be done. Everyone has something to offer, so ask yourself how you can apply your skills and passion to your child's school community.

82. Make Books Available

I cannot overemphasize the importance of reading. Reading expands the mind, builds comprehension, and prepares children with practical skills they can apply in the job market. Start early by making books available in your home. Also, ensure that you are helping your children develop a consistent habit of reading. If possible, have reading times just before bed so they can put themselves to bed with a good book. When your children are very young, read to them every night. Reading develops a life-long love of learning and strengthens the special bond between you. Take your children to the library, buy books online, ask the school or the teacher to recommend books. The goal is to ensure there are always books available to read in your home. One can never over-read or be over-educated. The more you read, the more you know, and the better you perform.

83. Reward Effort

Everyone is motivated by recognition and encouragement. Children, especially, love to feel special through recognition of their efforts. Be sure to give your child rewards for their effort and the things they do that you admire. Rewards can be verbal or tangible. Simple statements like, "you should be proud of yourself," or, "I am very proud of you," or, "great work, keep it up," go a long way toward making a child feel special about themselves. The better they feel, the more they will want to repeat the positive effort or behavior. Rewards can also be tangible, but you do not need to go overboard here. Children appreciate any meaningful gift; it does not have to be big or expensive. It can be as simple as one-on-one time with a parent. The main idea is to show them you notice what they have done, and you appreciate and celebrate them for it.

84. Teachable Moments

In the course of your day, as you spend time with your children, you will live through experiences that teach lessons. Do not ignore or dismiss these experiences because they provide valuable life lessons. When you are watching TV together, going grocery shopping, doing household chores, and going about your daily routines, you will learn some valuable lessons. Be sure to stop and have a chat with your children about what life lessons they can learn in life's daily moments. Young children often have many questions. Be patient and answer them all to the best of your ability. Do not ignore or dismiss their curiosities; this is how they learn and grow. Tell your child stories about heroes who have surmounted daunting odds. Talk to them about overcoming obstacles and what it takes to push through challenges. It is in these teachable moments that life lessons are learned.

85. Reward Good Grades

Good grades are not an easy feat to accomplish. It takes hard work and discipline to earn an A or B grade, so be sure to celebrate your child for their diligence. Show them how much you value good grades by talking with them anytime you see their grades rise or fall. Keep a constant dialog going about the importance of good grades and why they must maintain their grades. Talk to them about how and why to improve their grades when they drop; teach them techniques such as studying more, doing extra credit work, talking to the teacher, and being tutored. There is a whole range of things you can do to celebrate good grades. Sometimes a simple high-five will do, other times you may want to reward them with tangible or intangible gifts, but the most important thing is to acknowledge their success. Nothing succeeds like the feeling of success. It also lets your child know your expectations of success, and how much you value their educational success.

86. Chores

In today's technology-saturated world, many children are glued to the screen more than their homework. They spend their time playing video games, watching TV, browsing the internet, or chatting and texting friends. As a result, they do not contribute to household tasks. They do not clean their rooms or help out around the house. Be sure to assign chores to your child. Ensure that they clean their room, help prepare meals, clean the kitchen and different parts of the house, take out the trash, and run family errands. Be sure to acknowledge and praise them for doing their part. People will do more of what you want them to do when you recognize their efforts. Never take your child's effort for granted. You also do not have to do anything extreme to show them that you value their contributions in the home. A simple *"thank you"* is good.

87. Children's Programs

The library offers a broad range of programs for children of all ages. Take advantage of these programs, such as the various types of reading challenges offered. Inquire at your local library and enroll your child to take advantage of all the offerings. As a parent, you should never stop building your children's academic skills and exposing them to increased opportunities for learning math, language and the arts. These basic foundations are critical to their overall success and future goals. These programs also nurture your relationship with your children by offering you opportunities to bond and spend time together. There are also several offerings at local museums and other educational outlets. Let your children's minds explore; this is an excellent way to expand their unique life experiences and their thinking, as well.

88. Immunize

I have seen first-hand the impact lack of immunization does to a child. Babies are born with protection against certain diseases because antibodies from their mothers were passed to them through the placenta. After birth, breastfed babies get the continued benefits of additional antibodies in breast milk. But in both cases, the protection is temporary. Immunization (vaccination) is a way of creating immunity to certain diseases. Your child's doctor will determine the best vaccinations and schedule for your child. The American Academy of Pediatrics (AAP) recommends that children get combination vaccines (rather than single ones) whenever possible. Many vaccines are offered in combination to help reduce the number of shots a child receives. Check with your healthcare provider and be sure your child has taken all of their recommended vaccines to ensure optimal health and disease prevention.

89. Offer Academic Help

Sometimes you may feel confused or overwhelmed about how to help your child to perform better in school. If your child is struggling in school, ask the teacher how you can help out at home. Find out what your child's unique needs are, and what specific help you can offer them over and above their homework. What areas of the curriculum do they struggle with? Where could they benefit from additional help? Do they need a tutor to help further their understanding of these topics? Do they need extended school year services, like summer school? Do they need after school programs? Do they need you, as their parent, to sit with them for a few minutes a day and help them go through the specific things they need? To answer these questions, you must have a good understanding of how your child is performing in school.

90. After-School Programs

After-school programs are not for everyone, but if you feel your child needs the additional support, then you should consider enrolling them in one. There are benefits and drawbacks, depending on where the program is held. Some of them are more structured and organized than others, while some are more for enrichment support than academic support. Some offer homework help; others do not. Find out the nature of the program you are interested in and decide if you like the objective of it. Many programs offer additional reading, writing, and math help for students who need the support. Some of these programs do not provide practical help for students, so make sure you have a good idea of what is being offered in the program before you enroll your child in it. Parents who work all day have found it to be beneficial for their children, although the program should not be construed as babysitting support. Its primary goal should be educational support.

91. Reading Programs

Reading is the foundation of all learning. It is therefore essential to find specialized programs which can teach your child to be a better reader. These programs simply focus on reading and teach students how to increase their reading speed and gain mastery of reading fluency. Early reading skills prepare your child for advanced classes in high school and college, and for professional careers. Early reading skills are especially important for students who have a specific learning disability or other health impairment. Having your child in a reading program is a powerful way to build their reading and comprehension skills. There is no excuse to allow your children to struggle in reading when there are resources available to help. The inability to read can ultimately affect their self-esteem, and you do not want that.

92. Out-of-School Programs

It is a good idea to consider out-of-school programs when offering your child academic help. Some of these programs are paid programs, others are discounted, and some may be free. Find those that are within your means and enroll your child in them. Sometimes what the school offers may be limited; they may not offer what your child needs. An example of an out-of-school program is the Boys and Girls Club. Certain colleges also have classes for children in the summer. These classes range from hands-on to content instruction. They teach classes such as guitar, sewing, graphic design, and cooking, and also academic classes like math, reading, and writing. What a great way to expose your child to knowledge! Tutoring is also a great way to offer your child help with school work. Some of these are paid programs as well, although school districts sometimes offer free tutoring for underperforming students.

93. Discuss Favorite Subjects

One of the things that is so hard for many students to discuss is what they desire to do in a future career. One reason this is so hard for them is that they do not know the range of career options that are available. They only know the usual careers which they see around them, such as doctors, teachers, nurses, and police officers. If you wish to expose your children to an extensive range of careers, you must have conversations with them about what interests them. Chat with them often about what subjects they like. Examine how they perform in certain classes to discover which subjects they excel in and where their interests lie. When you discover this, do a Google search for possible exciting and well-paying careers that meet their interests. This is crucial in positioning your child for success.

94. Discuss Favorite Activities

Activities will become a huge part of your child's college and scholarship applications. Find out what interests your child and begin to help them develop their skills in those areas. Also, schools have clubs that your child can join. These clubs help students develop skills in unique niches. Colleges want to see what your child has been involved in, so be sure your child participates in extracurricular activities. Over the course of the summer, encourage your children to do community service – summer is best since they are so busy during the school year. Also, encourage them to start new hobbies, like sewing, gardening, recycling, singing, playing an instrument, and anything that gets their creative juices flowing. Colleges consider what children do in their spare time; some scholarships require participation in specific clubs and organizations.

95. Discuss Favorite Books

With the advent of technology and social media, books are beginning to be a lost art. A friend of mine once asked me, *"Why should I read books when I can just watch a video or listen to audio?"* That is, indeed, a great question. My answer is that books and videos each serve their purpose. Books expose and expand your mind in ways that video does not. For children, it improves their vocabulary, reading comprehension, and reading fluency. The truth is, reading for pleasure is a challenge for many students because they have so much homework and tons of reading to complete during school, especially in high school. After completing their school work, many children just want to rest and not pick up another book. Have a chat with them about what books they would like to read and what interests them. You can help your child develop an interest in reading by providing them with a favorite book on a favorite subject.

96. Discuss Books They Are Reading

Does your child love to read? If yes, that is great! Build on their interests by engaging them in discussions about their books. In a comfortable, relaxed setting, ask them what happened in the book they are reading, who were the characters in the story? Where did the story take place? When did the story take place? Why did the story happen? These questions get your children thinking creatively and expand their comprehension of the text. To get your child to play with the text, even more, invite them to write. They can either write on a writing template which you can download online, or they can write in their journals or a notebook. When children love books, they enjoy talking about the subject of their book to others, so ask away and let them express themselves!

97. Encourage

Every child needs support from their parents, such as hearing, *"I believe in you. I see your effort. Keep going. I am proud of you."* Encouragement means that you acknowledge your children's progress and effort, not just their achievement. Celebrate your child in their journey. If your child is struggling with an academic or life issue, let them know that you see their effort, and encourage them to give their best, instead of criticizing and blaming. Encourage your child to persevere through challenges, to see obstacles as an opportunity to grow, and as an integral part of their journey to success. Teach them that nothing worth achieving comes without struggle. By encouraging your child through their efforts and difficulties, you are also building resiliency in them and helping them defeat low self-esteem that discourages so many children and adults.

98. High School Courses

Talk to your child about their high school courses and verify that they are taking classes which will help them fulfill college entrance requirements. While an elective credit may be good in high school, it may not have the same relevance in college. Students in high school are encouraged to take a wide variety of classes, no matter the degree they want to pursue. Encourage your child to discuss their choices with their counselor, and to do their research to find out what class requirements they need for college admittance. The truth is, as long as a student is performing well in school, this process usually takes care of itself. School counselors are trained to direct students in what to do. Your primary job is ensuring your children maintain good grades and position themselves for college and beyond.

99. Discuss Careers

As a parent, you have good reason to be concerned about your children's financial future. Will they be able to live a comfortable life without financial struggle? Will they make good decisions about careers? Will they choose jobs that will satisfy them emotionally as well as financially? Will their financial decisions be able to sustain their mode of living and retirement expenses? Will they earn enough to support their own children's education? These questions should force every parent to think about their children's future. When you ask parents what they envision for their children's career future, they will tell you they want their children to be "happy." Happiness is great, but it is important to have a serious talk with your child about what happiness means to them and name the things that will make them happy. Financial security contributes to happiness in significant ways, so have a discussion about career choices often. If your child's choice is in a career field that does not pay well and they cannot meet their monthly bills, this could introduce stress in their lives.

100. Know their Friends

You need to know the friends who surround your child. You need to know where they live, who their parents are, and what their values are. Who are their friends' friends? The values and principles which you have taught your child are too important to be compromised by friends who do not share similar values. As a parent, you must ensure that you create a safe and comfortable home environment for your child. Many children want to run away from their home to their friends when they do not feel love, support, and encouragement from their family. Give your child a lot of love and support at home so they do not need to find it with friends – especially negative friends.

101. Part-Time Work

Many children feel that they need to work to make extra money while going to school. Sometimes they merely wish to earn extra money so they can take care of their needs instead of always asking their parents for money. If your goal is to help your child focus on school and climb the academic ladder, then you may want to talk to them about how working could counter that goal of academic success. High school and college can be extremely time-consuming and require intensive focus, concentration, and hard work. If your child's goal is to pursue a professional course of study, working a regular job may delay their completion of the program or impact their performance. Some students are highly organized and able to do both. It is a matter of personal preference and what your goals are, so choose wisely; think about your long-term goals vs. your short-term decisions.

102. Good Night's Sleep

Sleep is necessary for optimum brain function in children. Sometimes in class, I will ask a child a question that requires critical thinking, and because they are too tired, they cannot give me the answer. They will yawn, and sometimes they will say, "Ms. Ambe, I'm tired." Then I will ask, "When did you go to bed last night?" and they will say "Very late." Then I will ask "Why did you go to bed so late?" They will give me a variety of reasons: I was watching TV, or playing video games, or the music was too loud, or my parents were arguing. Your child needs *at least* nine hours of sleep each night. So much analytical thinking in school requires that children be awake and alert. Put your child to bed at eight p.m. to ensure they get enough rest, and wake up refreshed and rejuvenated to take on the school day.

103. Show Enthusiasm for their Work

Show excitement about your child's class work. Show interest in what they do each day. Ask them about their challenges. Listen intently and with interest as they discuss things that happened to them at school. Ask questions based on what they have told you and seek to extend the conversation so that your child can explain more. Help them create more study time and implement study skills. Stop in their study area to check on them and monitor their work; make sure they are on track and ask if they need your help with anything. Ask their opinion on school and the future, and where they want to go with their education. This level of interest will get them thinking seriously about the importance of school. Be excited about getting them school supplies and what they need to complete their assignments.

104. Resources for College

There are tons and tons of resources available online and through schools to help students accomplish their academic goals. Dig deep to find those resources and help your child take advantage of all that is out there. Google 'scholarships' and you will see a whole range of options. Go to my website at www.nicolineambe.com/scholarships to see a few that are available. For some of these scholarships, you simply register for an account and the company will then match you with scholarships for which you qualify. Sit down, or encourage your child to sit down, and apply for those which they qualify for. Make this a full-time job. Most of the requirements are easily doable. Gone are the days when applicants were required to submit all kinds of documentation. The process has been simplified, so take advantage of it!

105. Start Early

Your child's learning starts in the first five years of life. It is imperative to give them a good, solid, early start. Get your child reading early, speaking well, writing clearly, loving to learn, and ultimately succeeding in school by starting very early! The time to start is **now**! Children begin reading, writing and counting long before they go to school and what you do and say as a parent can give your child a great start. The good news is that you do not have to buy expensive games and books. It is what you do that matters. Talk to your baby often. Even when you feel they do not understand what you are saying, keep on talking. Use words that describe what you are doing. Use positive words. Read to your baby every day. Tell them a story or sing a song. Be intentional about teaching them through play.

106. Study Time

Create a formal study time at home. A time when everyone is reading or focused on learning something new, with or without homework assignments from school. I can almost hear you grumbling and saying you cannot find the time to do this because you have to work, and you have a busy schedule, and you have all these things you need to do. However, I cannot stress how important it is that you find the time! It can be daily, twice a week, or sometime during the weekend – whatever works for your routine. When you make study time a family value, you are conveying the message that reading is important in the grand scheme of life. You are exposing your child to more information and helping them learn through reading. This practice also creates a special bond between you and your child. It gives you something meaningful to do so your child is not veering into wrong activities.

107. Dialogue

Spend time during the day talking with your child. Be sure to listen with patience and love as they express their ideas with you. Enjoy daily conversations about everyday events. You will be surprised and impressed by your child's ability to think and reason. Many times, children do not get the opportunity to express themselves and share their ideas. Silence can lead to pent-up feelings, and your child may start to doubt the validity of their ideas. Give your child a voice. Give your child an outlet for positive self-expression. Find out what they know and do not know. Find out what they think about everyday happenings. Find out what excites them. Find out their opinion on current events. When you value your child's ideas, you value who they are. Parents and children need to set aside at least an hour a day to talk to one another – not on Facebook, or on the cell phone, but face-to-face. You need quantity to make quality time.

108. Monitor Homework

Homework is an important part of your child's success in school because it extends their understanding of the content which the teacher taught during the day. Be sure your child completes their homework. Students often get points for completing homework neatly, so check to make sure they are doing a legible job. To ensure that your child sees the importance of homework, create a quiet home environment where they can work. Provide them with quiet, private space to do their homework. Your child's homework is a priority, so understand this and make accommodations when guests come to your house to visit. Most of what is on your child's homework have been taught in class, so with focus and good study skills, they should be able to get through their homework on their own. If they need your help, you can intervene to help them understand the problem, but do not solve it for them.

109. Do Not Expect Perfection

As parents, our greatest desire is to see our children excel in life and not be failures. This desire can push many parents to expect their children to be perfect and to do things a specific way. Remember that in the journey of life, we learn as we go and everyone makes mistakes. It is okay to have high expectations for your child, but do not demand perfection. How you encourage them, and the tone you use, will determine whether you want growth in them or perfection. There is a fine line between high expectation and perfection. The difference lies in the willingness to forgive and overlook their mistakes. Do not yell at them because they did not meet your expectations, but correct them with love and show them how to do things differently. Be patient and focus on their effort; through encouragement, they will produce accurate results.

110. Model Good TV Habits

TV viewing can be detrimental to a child's learning if they are left to watch it without any restrictions. Monitor your child's TV habits, because too much has been known to affect children's health and brain function. Also, model healthy TV habits by watching shows that uplift you and your child. Unfortunately, many parents watch R-rated shows in front of their children, and the impact of this on their young minds is alarming when they come to school. Be careful what you watch in front of your children; it affects them in many ways. Also, listen to the vocabulary used in the shows which you watch in front of your child. Children repeat what they hear over and over, so you want to watch shows that help them speak and express themselves clearly using appropriate language expression.

111. Visit the Library

Visiting the library is just one of the many activities you can do to bond with your child. When they are young, take them to the library. A library visit is a great activity for the summer. Many libraries have amazing summer events and activities that add to student learning and enrichment. Throughout the year they have open access to their computers, where you and your child can browse educational programs. Libraries also carry a broad range of books that your child will enjoy reading. Most importantly, the library is the perfect place for your child to spend the morning or afternoon; it is an enriching environment which helps them glean the importance of reading. While you are there, speak to the librarian about upcoming events in the community. You will find the library is a great (quiet) place for older children to study, too.

112. Watch TV Together

Schedule times and dates to just enjoy TV together with your child. Enjoy movie nights with your family, where you get to throw a vanilla scented blanket on the floor and just tuck yourself and your child in there and watch a good movie. Do not forget the popcorn! These are precious moments that will leave lasting, lifetime memories for you and your child. Let your child choose the show that she would like to watch, and although you may not like the show, show interest in it. You just might enjoy it. Discuss the show you are watching. Ask what they would have done if they were in the position of any of the characters. Talk about life lessons learned from the show. Watching TV together with your child is one of those rare moments that life offers. So make sure you savor the moment and live it to the fullest.

113. Teach Self-Respect

Self-respect is one of those attributes that will help your child defeat negative outside influences. When your child knows who they are, values who they are, and respects themselves, they can never be easily swayed or influenced by negativity. Help your child develop a healthy sense of self by showing respect for who they are. When children have self-respect, it improves their ability to learn, love and be creative. It also helps your child to be happy and succeed in life because they are content with who they are. Self-respect often comes from getting a good education in school, combined with the love of parents. Make your home environment a place your child loves and wants to be. When children are happy in their home, they are satisfied with themselves. You can add to this by watching how you make your child feel at every moment.

114. Teach Respect for Others

Gone are the days of etiquette and respect for others, or so it increasingly seems. These days, so many children will bump into adults and not even say 'excuse me.' They do not say 'good morning' or even acknowledge the presence of someone else in the room. It is also getting easier to find children who have outright disrespect for their parents and people in authority, like teachers and principals. Teach your child to show respect for themselves and others. In this era where music, movies, and games glamorize foul language, disrespect, and anger when dealing with others, your child could be vulnerable to such influences. Make sure you know what they are listening. Also, catch incidences of rudeness and address them immediately when they occur. Teach your child proper manners, and make sure you model respect for others as well. Set realistic expectations for your child in regards to their behavior.

115. Humility Is Not Cowardice

Humility is a rare but very powerful trait. It is an unassuming attitude which is clearly distinguished from pride and boastfulness. You might ask, "Why should I teach my child humility when we live in a world where being self-centered and arrogant are almost a prerequisite for being taken seriously in business, sports, and politics?" Your goal as a parent it to be sure your child does not grow up to be offensive and obnoxious to others. There is beauty in observing and dealing with a "quiet storm." Someone who has a deep sense of self will pursue what they want but does so in a very unassuming way. Humility is not cowardice. It is bold and brave, without being prideful, boastful and loud. Make sure you teach your child where their real value comes from and give them opportunities to serve others.

116. Bravery and Courage

Helping your child develop courage is a character trait that will help them surmount life's inevitable obstacles. Having courage gives children the ability to stand up for themselves, to not be intimidated by anyone, and to develop the skills to 'hold their own.' Teach your child to be brave. Courage is developed by giving your child a strong spiritual foundation and core values. Be sure to have constant, open communication with your child, so they feel free to share what is going on in their life, and then you can offer suggestions on how they can handle issues and deal with problems. Build and nourish your child's confidence through knowing and doing what is right even when it is not convenient. Challenge your child to try new things and do things that they fear, to never give up when it is hard, and to understand that being hard is part of the process to reach the goal.

117. Together Online

The online world can be a dangerous place for children. There are countless news articles which refer to evidence of voracious predators lurking online to take advantage of children. In this era where children are increasingly computer and gadget-savvy, you want to be very sure you know what your child is doing online at any given time. Develop a habit of sitting beside your child if they must get online to acquire educational resources. Take the time to browse through them and see what is useful, and what can help advance their education. The truth is, there is a world of very helpful information online that can be life-changing, but there is also information that can harm your child. Be sure you sift through this information together and discover the info that can help your child.

118. Explore Useful Websites

At first, when you start searching the Internet it will seem very overwhelming. But, be patient with the process, and think about how these resources will help you provide the support your child needs to reach their next level of education. Create a directory of these resources for easy access so that you do not need to search every time, or better yet, bookmark useful links in your browser. Some amazing websites you could explore are: PBS.org/parents (parenting tips and advice), ReadWriteThink.org (useful resources for K-12), Scholastic.org/parents/ (tips on reading and books), scholarship websites like Fastweb.com (for 9th grade and above), ReadingRockets.org (strategies and ideas to enhance student's reading and comprehension skills), OxfordOwl.co.uk (for children ages 3-11), and KhanAcademy.org (math, chemistry, computer programming, SAT practice). These are handy and useful sites you should save to explore in the future.

119. Money Management

One of the courses or programs that is clearly lacking in most schools is financial management and literacy skills. Teaching children to manage money is a fundamental skill that will affect their lives in serious ways in the future. If your child does not learn the value of money and how to manage their income, they will become financially illiterate and fail in life. How many adults do you know who live paycheck to paycheck, who have more debt than assets, who cannot afford to put their children through college, or who cannot pay their home loan if they lose their job? That would be many people you know, right? Your child needs to learn how to manage money, so they do not become one of these people. Encourage them to save their money, but require them to use their savings to buy the little indulgences they want. They need to learn that they are not entitled to things.

120. Encourage Independent Work

As much as possible, allow your child to take independent responsibility for their work. Resist the urge to jump in and rescue them. Provide them with the right work environment and monitor them as they work. Supervise them as they perform a household chore to make sure it is completed. Allow your child to take the lead in doing things while you observe. Also, encourage them to pitch in ideas and suggestions. Do not reject their ideas or make them feel that their suggestions are not important. Independent work helps build resiliency in children. Show your child that you love and support them and watch as they strike out on their own. Part of being independent means they can do things on their own and figure out answers for themselves when you are not around.

121. Establish Rules

Ground rules are essential for operating any successful enterprise, including running a home. Establish a minimum of expectations for your home and children, because clearly defined rules make it easy for your child to align their behavior with your expectations. A great tip for rules is to keep it very simple. A long and complicated set of burdensome expectations just makes it daunting and frustrating for everyone. Use a positive tone and language to express those expectations. The whole idea of rules is to expect that the home is run in a respectable way; that people respect boundaries, respect each other, and respect themselves. Children must be taught how to: speak to adults and siblings with respect, have respect for other people's property, respect boundaries, and complete chores to ensure the home is run smoothly and represents a place of peace and safety.

122. Do Not Be Defensive

The school day is filled with incidences and mishaps. Teachers are constantly resolving disputes that either involve them or other students. Your precious child, who does no harm at home or whom you have never observed in a conflict, could very well be at the center of a conflict in school. Perhaps the teacher has called on you to complain that your child is the perpetrator. Your immediate reaction is to come to the defense of your child and argue that they did not do what they have been accused of doing. Resist the urge to come to your child's defense, even if they did not do it. Try to hear the whole story of what happened, form an objective opinion and get involved in an objective way. Have a conversation with your child about involving themselves in incidences that can get them in trouble.

123. Assign Chores

Doing household chores has many benefits – academically, emotionally, and even professionally. Chores are a great way to help a child take responsibility for their life. Not only do chores help them become more independent, but it also teaches them the value of hard work. Resist the urge to let your child skip chores to do homework. Schedule and write down tasks, so each family member knows what is expected of them. The most important thing about chores is consistency and ensuring that they are completed when they are due. Do not tie chores to punishments. Let your child know that doing chores is an integral part of running a successful family; it is an essential teamwork event which makes the home comfortable for everyone. Establishing chores requires discipline and consistency on your part, as well. To be effective, you must check that the chores are complete when they are due and that you do your part in completing chores as well.

124. Monitor Activities

Make sure the time your child spends outside of school, in your absence, is accounted for. Know what they are doing and who they are spending time with. Many children have been known to get involved with bad friends or situations that are not desirable for them because they were not supervised. If your child is going to be away from you for any length of time, make sure you know what they will be doing. Give them assignments to complete or projects to do and request they turn them into you when you return. Ask them to give you an account of the things they accomplished while you were away. Evaluate and provide feedback. Make sure you know who they are keeping company with, and verify they are with friends or adults who will be a positive influence for them, who will not harm them physically or emotionally.

125. Sharpen Listening Skills

Listening skills are essential in today's world. It is the first skill to aid in learning. As your child goes to school, you want to encourage them to listen in class. It is through listening that they learn new information. Many children have difficulty maintaining self-control in the classroom. They are distracted by friends, objects, and their surroundings. You need to tell your child to listen attentively in class because if they fail to grasp the information when it is taught, then they will have to read it on their own, which is a tall order for most children. Listening is a skill that will benefit your child in the real world. They will have to listen to their employees, their employers, or even listen to themselves. Teach your child to listen by encouraging and praising attentiveness. Maintain a quiet home and assign tasks that will require them to focus.

126. Sharpen Speaking Skills

Speaking skills are highly essential in today's world. Encourage speaking and communication by engaging in conversations with your child. Many children have a difficult time expressing themselves in class due to limited vocabulary and lack of exposure to proper communication. Be sure to find consistent opportunities to get your child to speak up about the things that are important to them. Find out what is happening in their life. Show interest in what they are saying. Restate ideas to indicate that you are listening. Provide positive feedback through facial expressions, gestures, and acknowledgment. Ask question to probe and prompt them to think a little deeper about issues. Talking to your child often, and listening to each other speak, are fundamental skills. Children will emulate those same skills in their relationships with others. By so doing, you are teaching them to effectively, eloquently and logically express themselves.

127. Quiet Place to Study

Children develop disciplined habits when they are given the right environment to complete their work. Create a quiet spot in your home where your child can complete their homework. Provide good lighting and a study table with tools, like paper and writing instruments. Remove all distractions, such as cell phones and Internet connections. Not only does this help your child stay focused on thinking through and completing their work, but it also teaches them discipline, attention, and getting the job done. One of the biggest problems I see with many children is a lack of attention – the inability to sit for an extended period to study and complete their assignment. That is partly because the environment is too busy and forces them to look around. When you create a quiet environment, you help your child develop good learning habits that will positively impact them.

128. Encourage Writing

The more your child writes, the better they will be as writers. One of the greatest challenges that children face in school today is putting pen to paper – writing. They have difficulties writing constructive paragraphs that explain a central idea with details. Three effective writing strategies will help your child enhance their writing abilities: copying, dictation, and narration. For copying, find a book, text, passage, lyrics, poem, or paragraph that is in the child's area of interest, or that is fun and exciting and have them write it word-for-word. For dictation, seat your child on a table and instruct them to copy the text verbatim on lined paper. For narration, read the selected passage slowly aloud so that your child becomes familiar with it. Ask your child to write down, in their own words, what you just read aloud to them. Practice these three strategies at home and you will have a great writer (and possible author) someday.

129. Work Space

Be sure to allocate a special place at home where your child can complete their homework. It is important that they take ownership of this space and that they understand the purpose of the space. Help your child realize the value and sanctity of a workspace; to realize that a workspace is a create space, a place where they get to focus on getting work done and being productive. This is a space where distractions do not happen, a place where they get to accomplish their goals and dreams. The beauty of assigning a workspace, or quiet place, to your child is they recognize the value of hard work and learn to develop a good work ethic. More importantly, they learn to focus on their work, and on what is truly important at that moment.

130. Parent Leadership

Strive to run your home like a leader. Leaders lead positively. Leaders inspire. They are not bossy. Leaders inspire people to take positive action to produce positive results. See parenting as team work where the responsibility of doing well does not just reside with your child, but with the entire family as a whole. Success becomes a family goal and a family expectation. When you lead, you brainstorm problems as they arise. When your child runs into problems, you can openly discuss the issues and seek ways to fix them as a family. You have to be the captain of the ship at home. Create trust and respect; show understanding and openness to the ideas of every member of the family. When you do that, you create a unit of people who work together and look out for the interest of each other.

131. Teach Good Money Habits

No matter how old or young your child is, it is essential to start teaching good money habits. Teach them how to save their money, and not spend it on things that will not bring them any return. Many people retire and do not have any retirement savings. Many people work, but still do not have money at the end of the month (although they have significant incomes). This lack is all because of poor money habits. People spend their money on anything and everything, and by the end of the month, or at the beginning of their retirement years, they have no money. It is important to teach good money habits to your child because this will make a tremendous difference in the quality of their lives as adults. Open up a checking account or savings account for your child and force them to use their savings to buy the little luxuries they want. They need to learn that they are not entitled to things like cell phones, computers, fashionable clothes, flat screen T.V.s, and so on. They will appreciate and care for things more when they must pay for them.

132. Model Good Money Habits

It is essential that you model good money habits for your child to emulate. Often, as parents, we get into spending habits that throw us into a financial quagmire. We seek to provide the best for our children and sometimes end up spending money on frivolities. For some, they just want to do what others are doing – a "keeping up with the Joneses" lifestyle. When children understand the value of money, they will be more careful about how to spend it. Children copy their parents' money habits, so unless you have disposable income, you want to teach your child to live within their means. Also teach your child to give to charity. Money does not always have to be spent on oneself or material goods; it can be used to help others who are less fortunate.

133. Life Beyond School

One of the most challenging things colleges experience is entering freshmen who are very unprepared for college life. These students are not able to take care of their own mental and emotional needs. They cannot deal with the pressures and deadlines, and they quite simply fall apart, having left the sheltered home environment. This can transfer to other aspects of life, where children are just not ready to take on the challenges of daily living. Be sure to teach your children resiliency. To do this, offer them simple chores to do at home consistently. Do not intervene to rescue them when you see them struggling with something. Let them take the initiative in problem-solving. Assign your child tasks and responsibility. Offer them leadership positions at home and make them assume responsibility for completing specific tasks. The idea is to keep them consistently in the doing mode, and not to be idling around doing nothing.

134. Limit Screen Time

There was a study done that showed poor people have poverty habits which keep them poor. One such habit is the uncontrolled use of cell phones, social media, and watching endless hours of TV. Limit your child's use of TV to no more than one hour at a time during the day. These forms of technology are a huge distracting influence in our lives and they prevent many children from reaching their academic goals. They even prevent many adults from doing things they said they would do. Take note of the substantial impact this has on your child's productivity; you need to create systems around how to enforce limits. The best thing you can do is require that your child replaces the screen with something else, such as listening to music, reading an entertaining book, completing their homework, playing outside, going to bed, or some other healthy or enriching activity.

135. Know the Teacher

At the start of the school year, find out who is going to be teaching your child. Be aware of their teaching style, their classroom management style, their knowledge of the content, and their personality. These factors will go a long way toward helping your child to learn. Learn about the teacher before or after they are assigned to your child and if there is something you do not like about them, ask for another teacher. There are no guarantees that your request will be honored but ask anyway. The right teacher will make all the difference in your child's learning and ultimately in their life. When your child has the right teacher, and you are happy with them, you need to keep your end of the bargain: ensure that your child pays attention and listens in class. Make sure they complete all their homework on time.

136. Reading Fluency

Require that your child read one or two educational books a month. This is is exactly what Ben Carson's mother did. He was labeled as the dumbest kid in his fifth-grade class and moved to the top of his sixth-grade class in one and a half years. Carson was raised by a single mother who spent her days and nights cleaning wealthy people's homes for money. She was depressed, divorced and illiterate. When she realized that she had a problem brewing in her home, she made her son read two books a month and submit a book report to her. She limited TV to 2 favorite shows a week. This paid off big time! Ben Carson became the head of pediatric neurosurgery at Johns Hopkins Hospital at age 33. He has performed breakthrough surgeries that have changed the lives of his patients. So, require your child to read!

137. Limit Junk Food

Limit junk food to no more than 300 calories a day. There is a direct correlation between a child's fitness and nutrition, and their performance in school. As a parent, you want to make sure you opt for healthy, nutritious meals, as far as your child's eating is concerned; this is better for brain development and clarity. It boosts their immune system and helps fight fatigue. It gives children energy and stamina to stay focused throughout the school day, whereas junk food drains their energy. Limiting junk food is especially important for children who have been diagnosed with ADHD and put on medication. Unfortunately, these medications impact children in many ways, one being they cause the child to be drowsy and fall asleep in class. For these children, healthy food choices will go a long way toward boosting their brain power and helping them stay active and engaged in the classroom.

138. Goal-Setting

Require that your child set monthly, annual and five-year goals. Goals give them a perspective of where they are going and what they are working toward. To do this, talk to them about their future and purpose in life. Talk about why goals are important and how they can make a significant transformation in their life. You also, as a parent, should have goals for your child. Setting goals ensures that your child stays on track and maintains a work habit that focuses on achieving those goals. Goal-setting is a powerful success habit. An example of a monthly goal would be, "Raise my grades in algebra." An example of an annual goal would be, "Raise my GPA to 4.0." And an example of a five-year goal would be "Go to college." Five-year goals will depend on what grade your child is in now, and what they want to accomplish for themselves.

139. Volunteer Work

Encourage your child to do volunteer work when they are of age. Any number of hours is good when it comes to volunteering, depending on your child's schedule. It is true the school week can get very busy with class work and assignments. When your child has some time off over the summer, make sure they are using part of their time to do volunteer work or even paid work. Some examples of volunteer work are: working at a park or summer camp; working at a hospital or clinic; babysitting a pet or a child. The list is endless. Use an internet search engine to find a list of possible volunteer opportunities for your child. Also, talk to friends, counselors, and people you know, about possible volunteer opportunities. Volunteering is great because it teaches your child essential work habits and also adds to their resume.

140. Save for a Rainy Day

We live in a consumer society, where it is trendy to spend. Teach your child to resist the urge to spend, especially on things that are not needs. Financial literacy and a good savings mentality elude many, so you want to make sure you teach this to your child, and that they save at least 25% of their income from earnings and gifts. As adults, they will need to understand the concept of paying yourself first. This means when you receive revenue from any source, you have to pay yourself first a portion of that income before you start spending it on other things. Many people find themselves at the end of their working years with not enough money saved. You want to teach your child good money savings habits early on so that they will know how to manage their money as adults. Money habits are critical to your child's happiness and peace of mind.

141. Relationships

Teach your child how to build and nurture relationships. Relationship building is key in making connections as they go through their years of school, college, and career. Your child will need valuable relationships with people who can help them get what they desire in school and life. Relationship building will also help them learn to interact with people in social and workplace settings. To help your child in this, require them to call friends, teachers, and family members on their birthdays. Also, require them to send thank-you cards for gifts or help they receive from anyone. Encourage your child to call and check up on friends and family that are sick, and to send cards. An important part of this is stopping by for a random visit with someone. One-on-one interaction is key. The ability to make connections will help your child develop a vital skill called networking.

142. Fail First

Reassure your child that mistakes are okay, and not bad. So many children feel discouraged and bummed when they fail a test or fail to meet a target. Children need to understand that the very foundation of success in life is built on learning from our mistakes. Whenever you see your child sad because they made a mistake or feel they have not met an expectation, use that as a teaching moment to reassure them that the essence of learning is to find out what we do not know, and then work to know better. If everyone knew the answers, there would be no such thing as learning. We learn from our mistakes, and we learn because we do not know. As a parent, you also need to have a good attitude about failure, and a good response to it when you see your child struggling. Mistakes are part of life; do not make them feel worse about it.

143. Temper Anger

Punish children when they lose their tempers so they understand the importance of controlling this very costly emotion. Demonstrate appropriate emotional responses to situations yourself. Children learn behaviors by watching their parents; if your responses are usually violent outbursts, your child will learn to react in the same way when faced with a similar situation. Encourage calm through conversation and teach your child to keep things in perspective. Temper flare-ups can land your child in troubled waters and cause them to lose their relationships with others. They can even land them in jail. In any setting – in business or the workplace – it is essential to control an emotional response to a situation. It is always wise to think through a situation before responding.

144. Money is no Vice

Teach your child that seeking financial success in life is a good and worthwhile goal. Children need to learn what the American Dream is and that it is something to be pursued in life. Too many people look down on money and wealthy people, yet money is the very reason many of us go to work. 'Wealth' is simply the acquisition of money without sacrificing your family and relationships. Too many families are struggling with debt, struggling to make ends meet, and living from paycheck to paycheck. Having enough money will make a tremendous difference in your child's life. Having enough money will provide them numerous opportunities to make financial choices without stress. They can buy the house and car of their dreams, go on vacation where they want and have enough extra money to give back to charity. As a parent, you want your child to do better than you. You want to pass on blessings, not curses. So, see them as the successful young men and women that they will eventually become.

145. Time Management

The world is increasingly busy. Too many social interactions and stimulation are causing children to fall short in school and miss academic targets. This is a tremendous problem. Teach your child how to manage their time. They should be required to create daily "to-do" lists, and these lists need to be monitored by a parent. The goal should be to accomplish at least 70% of the tasks on their daily "to-do" list. Having a daily to-do list is a habit for the world's most successful leaders. You want your child to be able to lead themselves, and not be led by the events around them. You want your child to have a good sense of direction; to know what they want and get on the path to getting what they want, instead of losing track and losing direction as a result of distractions from situations and circumstances around them.

146. Plan for PTCs

Parent-teacher conferences are designed to keep parents up-to-date on their children's academic performance. They help parents find details and information on their children's behaviors and attitude at school and towards school. I encourage you to attend your child's parent-teacher conference to learn more about your child's disposition toward school. You will be very surprised what you learn, and you may discover a side of your child that you never knew existed. Many children show one personality at home and something completely different at school. Be sure to write your questions out ahead of time to ensure that you do not forget anything during the conference. When and if you disagree with the teacher, make sure you are positive in disagreement: remain calm, avoid anger, and find facts for yourself. Make sure your child is not causing problems for the teacher; make sure they are on track and doing what they are asked to do in class.

147. Enjoy Life

Remember, your child benefits when you are the best version of yourself. Take time to empower yourself so you can inspire your child. Never sacrifice critical areas of your life for less important ones. Remember that you can be healthy and emotionally fulfilled, experience success at work, and have fulfillment at home. You *can* have it all! Critical aspects of your life include work, relationships, health, and self. All of these areas of life are crucial to ensure that you are balanced and emotionally sound. Many parents are out of balance. Some work too hard and forget to spend time with their children. Others focus so much on their children or work and forget that self-care and health are critical to their wholeness. Make sure that you give due diligence to your job, that you nurture positive relationships that enrich your soul, that you pursue and achieve ultimate health, and that you take care of yourself emotionally.

148. Attend Events

Over the course of your child's academic life, they will likely have numerous extra-curricular activities, field trips and other performances that will demand their time and talent. As you know, these events build your child's self-esteem in school and contribute positively to their overall wellbeing. So, support and encourage the best in them. Attend their sports events and concerts. Cheer loudly and proudly from the stands. If you cannot attend, show them support in other ways at home. Tell them how proud you are of them. Tell them about courage, and about pursuing their goals, and staying laser focused. Tell them about being the best, and to develop work habits that position them to move to the top of whatever field they choose to pursue. Never put your child down or denigrate their efforts. That will just defeat and deflate them. Be positive and encouraging through your words and physical presence.

149. State Testing

Talk to your child about the rationale for tests. Tell them that tests are designed to discover their subject-matter knowledge. The results of tests position students for opportunities later in life. How your child performs on any test is crucial to their academic livelihood and the opportunities that they will experience. The global market is increasingly very competitive, so your child's performance on the state test will either help them be able to compete in the job market and cause them to miss out on opportunities. Talk to your child about test-taking strategies such as taking the time to read carefully before answering a question, and not rushing through their work. Ensure your child is well-rested before a test. Help them avoid test anxiety by calming them down. Do not stress about test scores or pressure them, but expect strong performance from them. Review incorrect answers on tests and help point out their mistakes so they can correct them next time.

150. Position for Scholarships

Getting scholarships for college does not just happen in twelfth grade. It happens way before twelfth grade, as early as third grade. How your child performs in math in third-grade will determine how they will perform in math in middle school – which further determines how many scholarships they will get for college. Certain subjects qualify students better for scholarships than others. Math and science, engineering, and technology courses rank high for scholarships. Position your child for these opportunities by ensuring they have mastery of basic facts in early grades and continue to maintain that proficiency through high school. Scholarships come with good grades and specific subjects.

151. School Attendance

School attendance is critical to your child's success. When students miss school, they miss out on crucial content that will make a tremendous difference in their academic performance. Several students have the misfortune of moving around from school to school to school. By age 12 some students have moved through 5 schools or more. Such change is not good at all for their performance. Make sure that your child attends school regularly. Also, ensure that they do not come to school late. Too many tardy marks will affect a student's attendance and cause them to possibly lose credit for work completed. When students come to school on time and attend regularly, they learn. Encourage them to listen and participate in class, ask questions to clarify concepts, and complete their homework. These are the critical elements of academic success.

152. Model Good Relationships

How you treat your spouse, and other relatives and friends, will profoundly influence the way your child treats others, so model respectable relationships. Teach your child respect for self and respect for others. Help your child understand that relationships are an important part of life and encourage them to take the time to nurture meaningful relationships with loved ones and close friends. Help your child understand that relationships can help them deal with tough situations. When you treat others with respect as a parent, when you model good rapport with family members and friends, your child will learn to do the same. Be careful how you speak *to* others in front of your child; be careful how to speak *about* others with your child. You are the primary person they look to as an authority on how to treat others and how to be treated by others.

153. Set Personal Goals

Goals help people accomplish things that they would like to achieve in their lives. As a parent, you likely have a vision for your life and your children's lives. You likely have things that you would like to achieve and would also like your children to accomplish. Everyone needs to have that vision. Without that vision, life becomes meaningless. The best way to reach your dream is to develop goals and targets that help you get to the place that you see in your mind's eye. Be ruthless about achieving your priorities by setting daily goals to help you get there. What health goals do you have? What parenting goals do you have? What work goals do you have? What goals do you have regarding self-care? Set specific daily targets and work to meet them.

154. Avoid Self-Defeating Behaviors

Teach your child to avoid self-defeating thoughts. Self-defeat is a terrible attitude for anyone who wants to achieve success. Any successful person understands that they must have a deep sense of confidence in their abilities. They must believe that they have the qualities and skills to achieve their dreams and goals. They must refuse to take "no" for an answer in the process of working towards their goals. The world is already tough as it is, so you do not want to defeat yourself before the world gets a hold of you. Teach your child that they have what it takes to succeed. Many children feel bad about themselves; they feel inadequate, they do not believe in their gifts, and as a result, they do not feel that they are good enough. They, therefore, do not apply themselves. Counter this poor attitude by encouraging your child's strong belief in themselves through words of empowerment.

155. Have Empathy

Teach your child to show empathy for others. Teach them to put themselves in other people's shoes, and to reach out to others. Teach your child to love and care for others. Teach them to support you as a parent, and feel the way you feel regarding working hard to ensure that they get their needs met as children. Teach your child to care for their siblings. If your child is older, perhaps they could read to their siblings or help them with math. Assign chores so that they learn a communal spirit by understanding that a home is a community, and we all have to play a part to help it run smoothly. Chores help children develop grit, but they are also a good way for children to serve others by doing things that make life comfortable for others.

156. Be Assertive

If you have a child who is struggling or has special needs, be assertive about asking for what will help your child achieve their academic and life goals. Every resource or service goes a long way, so ask. If you fail to ask, you may not receive the support you need to help your child. Speak to the school principal about after school programs, summer school programs, and community and state resources that will assist your child further their education. Talk to friends or family that may be in the same or similar situation as you, and inquire about what resources or support they have. Plug into a support system that you feel comfortable with and that understands the unique needs of your child. Talk to teachers and seek mentors who show good will and want to help.

157. Model Appropriate Social Skills

Several studies show that students spend a lot of time on social activities, sometimes at the expense of their school work. The advent of technology has not made this easier; with so many video sharing apps and hangouts, students are spending more and more time on their devices. Be sure to find out what your child is doing on the internet and who they communicate with. Many adults disguise themselves as children online, so it is important to talk to your child about the risks of communicating with people they do not know. Also, speak to your child about appropriate behaviors when they go out with friends. As a parent, you have to model appropriate socialization skills as well. If you are loud and obnoxious at a party, you cannot expect your child to behave any differently. In fact, you are embarrassing your child.

158. Do Not Label Your Child

Labeling your child, or calling them names, is the worst and most awful thing you can do to your child. In fact, many of my students who receive special education services do not like being labeled as "special." Every child loves to be a normal child who does things normal children do. As much as possible, treat your child like any other child, even if they have a disability. Do not make them feel victimized. Use words of encouragement consistently to get them to believe that they are good enough, and you love them just the way they are. Confidence and self-worth are essential to success, so be sure to boost your child's confidence by not making them feel inadequate. We are all unique and beautiful in our own way. Your child may do things and act in ways that you do not like, but be patient and accept them for who they are while guiding them to be their best self. Do not criticize harshly or unjustly. Give feedback instead.

159. Relax

Parents tend to panic and act out of anxiety when their child does not produce the way they expected. Often children fail to meet their parents' expectations or reach their personal goals. Perhaps they fail in school, earning D and F grades. It is easy to feel stressed when your child fails to meet your dreams and goals for their life. Relax and take things in stride. Remember that F.A.I.L. means "First Attempt In Learning." I have come to learn that life is about failure and learning from our mistakes. When you see your child struggling with something, pull back and find out how you can calmly help them get back on track. You cannot support your child from a place of panic and anxiety. It just adds more stress to you and your child. Calm down and take small but meaningful steps to address the issues that confront you.

160. Affirmations

Success comes from belief – a strong, firm belief in one's self. Where that belief is missing, affirmations help students discover the beauty, talent, and genius that lie within them. Encourage your child to say daily affirmations. Use my book, **Innate Genius**, available for on Amazon.com. If your child is younger, read it together and ask questions about what they have read. If they are older, gift them a copy to read for themselves, and invite them to share the principles learned. Also, do the exercises at the end of each affirmation to solidify the principle taught. The more frequently your child says affirmations, the more they will believe in them and start to affirm their self-worth.

161. Model Courage

Help your child develop courage. Courage is fearlessness and boldness. Boldness to speak up and ask for what you want; boldness to say what you want to say without caring how others perceive you; boldness to go after your dreams without letting others intimidate you or cause you to doubt your choices. Model the courage to be yourself without feeling inadequate; to tell the truth and face your consequences. Many children hide things from their parents and do things behind their parent's backs. Teach your child to never be afraid, to never be something or someone they are not. Teach them to be accountable for the things they have said and done. Encourage them not to tell lies and own up to their mistakes. Help them own the courage of their convictions.

162. Avoid Pity

Discourage your child from harboring feelings of self-pity. Self pity can lead to depression in later years. Guard your child against depression. In today's society, many children suffer from depression; they are being bullied at school or feel that they do not have friends, or feel like they do not belong. Eliminate all feelings of pity. Encourage your child to always see the bright side of life. Speak to them positively and with enthusiasm so they see the joy of living and just being themselves. Do not victimize them. Do not feel sorry for them when something happens or when they struggle with something. Instead, show them that life is about bouncing back. Talk to them about life struggles and how these struggles are a fundamental part of living. Share with them that life has seasons – a season to be sad and a season to be happy – but each season gives way to the next as life goes on. Life is about experiences and change – that is the nature of life.

163. State Test Preparedness

The best solution to ensuring your child's successful performance on future state tests is to stay involved in their education from the very beginning. The best time to prepare for the test is not the day or the week before the test; it is the months leading up to the test. Stay on top of your child's performance and see that they master grade-level standards. If you notice your child struggling with concepts, intervene immediately to fix them. Ask the teacher or find a tutor for your child. Sadly, many parents wait until the end of the school year before they start to pay attention to their child's school performance. At this point, it is too late, and all the standards have already been taught. Stay on top of your child's performance from day one and keep track of their grades.

164. Standardized Testing Tips 1-5

1. Do a fifteen-minute daily review of basic facts to help your child master math and reading fundamentals.
2. Make sure your child is reading to themselves and aloud to you daily. Children gain reading fluency and reading comprehension skills when they are exposed to literature.
3. Before the test, expose your child to practice questions, which you can get from your child's teacher or download from the Internet. Practice allows your child to become acquainted with a variety of test questions.
4. Coach your child to pay close attention to directions on the test, and highlight keywords that will help them answer the questions.
5. In multiple choice questions, students should eliminate the obviously wrong answers – the answers they know for sure are incorrect.

165. Standardized Testing Tips 6-9

6. The day before the test, and even the weeks leading up to the test, ensure that your child has a good night's sleep.

7. The weeks leading up to the test, be sure your child is eating healthy, nutritious meals that nourish their brains. A good breakfast on the day of the test is an excellent brain booster.

8. Make sure that your child attends school during the testing period. Do not plan any doctor visits during that time, unless it is an emergency. The school schedules make up tests, but these makeups may affect your child's morale.

9. Talk to your child's teacher and the school administrator about any concerns you might have.

166. Avoid Over-Protection

Our first instinct as a parent is to protect our children and give them the best that life can afford. Every parent wants to see their child happy and not hurt. We go the extra mile to give them what they need. However, too much can be too much. You cannot do so much for your child that they cannot do for themselves. Give your child the opportunity to explore new things; to take some risks in life. It is not always necessary that you must intervene to do things for them or bail them out. They need to develop grit and resilience, which prepares them to take on the challenges that life will dish out. Part of helping them develop the habit of taking risks is to assign chores at home and give them things to do and tasks to complete. Ensure that they finish these tasks to your satisfaction.

167. Be a Mentor

I cannot begin to tell you how many people I have met over the years who suffer from a deep lack of confidence, mental illness, emotional trauma, and low self-esteem, all as a result of something their parents said to them or did not say to them, did to them or did not do to them. Some even live in huge mansions and drive fancy cars, but still, suffer from the effects of mental and emotional abuse by their parents. They blame their parents for the bad things that happened to them and the way they feel. If you are a parent, I have a question for you. Is this you? If so, you should consider changing the way you speak and act towards your child because it could affect the way they feel. Nurture your child's sense of self and help them develop a deep-seated belief in themselves. Always use encouraging words – words that make them feel valued. Help them see the possibilities that lie within them and teach them they can achieve any goal through hard work, grit and perseverance! Do not be a dream killer. Be the kind of parent who inspires your child's hopes and dreams!

168. Take Your Child to Work

Employers often offer "take your child to work" days for their employees. If you have this opportunity, use it. This is an excellent way to spend time with your child in a new and unique environment that is different from the usual ways you would otherwise be with them, such as park days and other social opportunities. Use these work visits as teachable moments. Teach your child about respect for a business environment, work ethic, using time wisely, being a good employee, and give their best at work every day. Instill in them how doing well in school results in the job or career of their dreams. In essence, use the day as a learning experience and make sure to assign them work to help you – this is not a day for them to just sit around. Make them work and use their time there wisely.

169. Encourage Entrepreneurship

Entrepreneurship is something that comes easily to some children. Your child may be the type who loves to experiment and naturally wants to use their gifts. Encourage them, if that is what they want to do. Many people have made themselves millionaires by simply exploring their gifts and taking them to the next level. Several have done so without even pursuing a college degree. They simply have used their imagination to make money in creative ways. If you see your child working to start a business or put a skill to use for money, support them. You never know where their creative genius may take them. Also, it is okay to both go to school (and excel) and pursue a passion or business which you love. If your child loves photography, computers, sewing, or any unique activity, and wants to take that talent to a higher level as an entrepreneur, encourage them to do so.

170. Acceptance and Love

Accept and love your child for who they are. Have an open relationship which honors their needs and desires, but also places expectations on them. Truly, the purpose of life is to love those we hold dear and to make them feel special, to develop a meaningful relationship with them. Be intentional about creating this kind of relationship with your child. Have non-judgmental conversations with them, and listen to their point of view; make them feel heard. Pick your battles and do not be quick to point out their flaws. Skepticism only makes them feel inadequate or unworthy of your approval. Instead, encourage them. Empower them. Tell them they can be, do, and have anything in life because they have the capability. Teach them to recognize their talent and love themselves for who they are.

171. Break Tasks into Small Steps

When assigning your child a task, break it task up into small pieces. Do not ask them to do too many things at once. Ask them to do one thing at a time. Chunking ensures that they get the work done. Too many instructions can not only reduce the importance and urgency of what needs to be done, but it can also confuse your child as to what to do next. You want your child to start a task and finish it, and not leave work hanging. So assign one thing and a deadline and check that off when it gets done. Then move on to the next task and ensure that it gets done. This is how you do more in a very limited time. You may appear desperate if you try to make them do it all at once. Too much information can bbbe confusing for them and overwhelming for you.

172. Catch Them Doing Good

Catch your child doing good! Do not always expect to scream and yell at your child for not doing what they are supposed to do, or find fault and blame them for wrongdoing. Look for opportunities where they are doing something amazing, and celebrate them for that! Give them rewards for doing good work, such as when they move their grades up, clean their room, or show focus on their school work. The truth is, most people perform well when they are celebrated, when they feel appreciated for giving their best. The same goes for children. Do not just criticize – celebrate! Appreciation provides them with added motivation to do more of what is acceptable. Most children also want to please their parents, so they will do more of what they think makes you happy. Help them out by showing them what makes you happy – point out the good things they do.

173. Set High Expectations

When I speak to a group of parents, one of the usual questions I ask my audience is, "How many of you believe that your child is capable of success?" Almost all hands go up. Yet, we see many children who are struggling in school, who are falling behind, who are dropping out of school. Why is that? It is because, although some parents believe that their children are smart, they still have hidden doubt and unbelief about their child's ability to excel. They are afraid to "put pressure" on their children because they are not sure their children can do the work. Doubt what I call a parent's "limiting belief system." Do not let your limiting beliefs lower your expectations of your child. Have high hopes and expectations of your child because you *know* they are capable of achieving. When you have high expectations and create a learning environment that will help your child succeed, there is no doubt they *will* succeed!

174. Address Fears

FEAR – the word that kills all hopes and dreams, destroys even the most talented human being, stops people in their tracks, and causes a dreamer to deny the possibilities that exist in their lives and future. As a parent, you have to do all you can to address your children's fears. You need to have frequent conversations with your child to find out what is holding them back, then address those fears and limitations. It is essential to do this very early when they are children because it will affect them as adults. There are many adults today whose parents never addressed their fears or boosted their self-esteem. As a result, they struggle with several aspects of their lives. Take time to talk to your child about fear as just an illusion. Teach them that if they face the things which they fear, they will conquer their fears. Teach them to move past self-doubt and actually, do the thing they want to do. Fear dissipates with action.

175. Discuss Heroes

Are there any significant people in your life who have made a tremendous difference in how you think? Do you know individuals who have overcome insurmountable odds and obstacles, and you are just amazed that they were able to do it? As you look back over your life, are there events and things that happened to you that were quite challenging and now you are proud that you came through them? We all have challenges and setbacks, both large and small. The fact that you did not fall or let it set you back means you have courage in you. Share these stories of bravery and heroism with your child. Help them put suffering and hard times in perspective and understand that it is all part of life and living. Teach them never to fall prey to hard times, but to always develop the courage to pick themselves up and continue walking with purpose.

176. Persistence

What is your reaction when faced with difficulties and setbacks? Do you break down and react emotionally? Give up and quit? Or, do you live a life that is beyond your true essence, feel depressed and sad, or worse, let it affect the people around you? Your children learn persistence, resistance, and resilience by watching you. You must show character in times of trouble. Teach your child this unique attribute of persistence by talking to them about it, and *being* about it as well. Remind your child that life will have its set of difficulties around the bend, but they must persist and stay on their journey when faced with a roadblock. No one promised there will be no setbacks in life. It is unreasonable to expect life to be exactly as we would like it. Your child must learn to know and pursue their heart's desires, and to stand steadfastly persistent when they encounter difficulties which threaten their heart's desire.

177. Dreams

As a parent, you have dreams for your children. You want them to be happy and excel in life. The more you think about it, you want them to live a certain exemplary life that you can be proud of as a parent. Imagine if your child dreamt the same dreams that you have for them; their lives would reflect all that you envision for them. Sadly many parents run into resistance from their children when they try to dream for them. Your role as a parent is simply to paint a vision for your child, to teach them to take independent responsibility for their work, and to hold themselves accountable for their successful future. Teach them about life, and to create a home environment that positions them for success. When you successfully help your child take ownership of their life and their future, you have given them firm ground to stand on and wings to fly.

178. Be Amicable with Your Partner

How you treat others will have a direct influence on the kinds of relationships your child has with those around them. How you treat your relatives and co-workers will impact your child's behavior towards others. More importantly, how you treat your spouse/partner will be crucial in how your child values marital relationships or partnerships with others. Notice the way you talk to and interact with your partner or spouse when your child is present. Notice the way you talk to and interact with your partner or spouse when your child is *not* present. At all times, you must show the highest respect for your partner or spouse. Even if there are things which they have done that you do not like, express your feelings in a civil way. In other words, be civil but be honest. Be amicable, be cordial, and be honest with your partner or spouse every time.

179. Apply for Special Services

One of the beautiful things about living in America is the possibility which exists to make choices which will move your life forward. There are numerous opportunities available for those who desire to seek out the resources they need to make a significant improvement in their lives. There are grants, financial aid, and scholarships for students to complete college. There are business resources for those who want to start and run businesses. There are internships and volunteer opportunities for those who are starting a career or want to gain new skills that will give them leverage to pursue their ideal career. Whatever support your child needs to take their dream to the next level is available in the form of some service offered in the community. You and your child must seek out the opportunities that will help them further their options in school and career. But you have to be dedicated and want it badly enough.

180. Ask Questions

As a parent, you have to ask many questions to accurately guide your child. Ask questions of the school administrator, ask the school counselor about your child's college requirements, ask your child's teacher about how to help them do better in school or improve their grades. Contact potential colleges to ask about requirements and school offerings to see if your child is on track for admission. To help your child, you have to be fully present. You have to be an involved parent who knows exactly what is going on and can make informed decisions that position your child for success. Sadly, many parents wait until the last minute before finding out what they need to do help their children excel. Sometimes it is too late because the deadlines have passed. Be on the alert and ask questions. You also want to teach your child that asking questions will help them get what they want in life.

181. Parental Rights

You have rights as a parent, especially if you have a child with special needs. The school has an obligation to honor your right to make decisions regarding your child. As a parent, you know your child best; you know what your child needs to be successful in school and life, and you need to identify those opportunities and pursue them. Having rights as a parent does not mean you should be forceful and unreasonable. Do not be the parent who comes into the school and causes a scene about what needs to be done regarding their child. Nor the one who files sustained lawsuits demanding services and special treatment of their child. Remember that when you confront the school unreasonably, your child is watching you, and two things can happen. Your child will either behave like you or depend on you to help them get away with things.

182. Pass on Blessings, Not Curses

As a parent, you are supposed to pass on blessings, not curses. Start to see your child as the successful man or woman they will eventually become. Have high expectations; want more for them. There is a huge difference between insistently imposing your views and acknowledging what your child wants. Encourage your child to strive for more and to want to reach their next level. You could be living with an aerospace engineer in your home or a neuro-surgeon, but if you do not believe your child can do it, you will not help them reach higher. No matter what your background is, no matter what challenges you have as a family or as a person, always expect more from your child. Pass on the blessing of success, not the curse of the poverty cycle.

183. Work Hard

Success is never handed to anyone on a silver platter. You have to put in the work. "Work" is non-negotiable when it comes to success. To improve your skills, to get better at anything, you have to work hard. You have to work extremely hard to move your grades up; you have to work extremely hard to gain the skills you need to win the job of your dreams. Teach your child the value of a good work ethic. Teach your child to be conscientious of their work, and to take pride in their work. Teach your child not to be afraid of hard work, but to see work as an essential part of living. Work keeps your brain active, and it also enables you to feed your family. Teach your child not to see work as a problem but as essential to making them smarter. Work fills an important role in life.

184. Health Conscious Lifestyle

Your child is not too young to begin living a healthy lifestyle. Things that people do when they are younger carry over to when they are older. How you eat now will show up in your later years. If you eat junk foods when you are young, it will show up in your health when you are older. Unhealthy eating is how people develop heart disease and other ailments that cause their health to struggle. Be sure to encourage your child to eat healthy servings of protein, vegetables, healthy fats and fruits. Teach them to avoid foods like sugar, bad carbohydrates, etc. There is a wealth of information on the Internet on nutrition and healthy recipes. Elect to have a smoothie every day to ensure that your body has the nutrients in needs to carry you through the day. Drinks lots of water; around 2 liters will keep your child hydrated.

185. Dental Visits

It is amazing how many children struggle with dental issues at a very early age. Begin teaching your child good dental hygiene before they can even hold a toothbrush. Teach them to brush their teeth twice a day or after every meal. I have witnessed dental issues translate to total body health. Tooth decay has been known to cause other health-related issues as well, such as cardiovascular problems and vision problems. What your child does now regarding their health will catch up to them in their in their 40s and 50s. As a parent, you need to take on the role of a health coach and mentor for your child. Teach them the right health habits and help them live healthy and free from disease as they get older. Be sure to plan regular visits to the dentist and practice good dental hygiene on the daily basis. Ask your child's dentist for details on how to do this.

186. Teach Godly Morals

Increasingly, we live in a world where everyone wants to look and behave like the next person. With the advent of social media, people's private lives are no longer private, but out in the open. Most people are sharing aspects of their lives with the world, through pictures and writing, that they would not share with their neighbor in person. The tendency for those who are watching is to unconsciously start to replicate these behaviors. Social consciousness plays a huge role in altering minds and affecting actions. As a parent, you want to make sure that the values your child exhibits are not the result of having been swayed by social media, but are formed by their beliefs in life. Teach your child to know God and to obey His principles, to use those principles to make informed decisions in their lives. Take your child to a place of worship and involve them in church activities. By interacting this way, they learn healthy habits and godly morals.

187. Nurture Grit

Grit is what will get your child through tough periods. No matter what your child may face in life, no matter how difficult a task or challenge may be, having grit will help them withstand and overcome any adverse situation. Children who are pampered and spoiled never get the opportunity to handle serious challenges because their parents are always intervening to make things easy for them. You need to encourage your child to be independent at a very early age. Teach them to do chores around the home as young as five years old. They can be mommy and daddy's little helper, working along with you to do things. They should be able to do the dishes and their laundry by age nine. They should be able to make light snacks and meals in the kitchen at this age, as well. All these activities prepare your child to take on challenging situations in the real world.

188. Encourage Curiosity

Too often, parents will unconsciously censor their children. They stop their child from asking questions or even exploring new actions and ideas. We are all guilty of this as parents. But you must learn to allow you child to explore their curious mind. Human beings learn by curiosity – asking questions, investigating, wanting to know more, looking for answers to solve a puzzle. A curious mind is one which seeks solutions. If you have a child who is curious, who likes to try new things, who gets into things, allow them to do so within reason. The concern for most parents is their child's safety, and that is paramount. If safety is your concern, be present while they explore so you can guide them and keep them safe. If your child wants to try a new recipe in the kitchen, let them! You may have to clean up a mess (or teach them to), but they will learn a valuable lesson in cooking.

189. Enthusiasm

Enthusiasm is a fabulous trait in any human being. It is what gets people going and accomplishing what they desire. Everybody loves to be around enthusiastic people; those who are happy about life, and who are happy about what they are doing and accomplishing. To help your child develop enthusiasm in any area of life, you need to be inspiring and empowering for them. You have to show them the bright side of life. You have to be an enthusiastic person yourself because we feed off each other's energy. If you are someone who is always depressed and complaining, someone who has a gloomy outlook on life, that is the energy your will pass on to your child. Be enthusiastic and teach your child to love their work, to pursue a line of work that they are passionate about. Teach your child to seek the things in life that they love and to live their lives happy.

190. Conscientiousness

There are concerns that the current generation is self-centered. I tend to believe it is not their fault, but the era in which they are growing up. With the advent of social media, everyone is thinking about how to promote their own agenda. People have become selfish and self-centered. Children's attention spans are limited as there are a thousand and one things to do every day. Teach your child that they can develop empathy for others and be conscious of and conscientious about how they treat people in a world which is extremely busy. Conscientiousness even trickles down to the workplace and the job market in regards to how we treat each other. Teach your child that there is enough abundance in the universe for everyone, and it is not necessary to run people down and make them feel bad to get what you want. Teach them to develop a charitable mindset – a mindset of giving to the poor, the sick, and the less fortunate.

191. Self-Control

Self-control is the ability to maintain poise and discipline over happenings that occur in our life, and not be swayed or influenced by them. As human beings, self-control is very important to master. Teach your child to know and understand who they are, and what they are capable of, so they are not easily influenced or controlled by forces outside of themselves. A natural way to teach this is to be present for your child, to maintain a stable home, and to create a routine which helps your child keep order in their life. Lack of self-control in children is often the result of living in a disorganized environment with no predictability or calm. It could also be the result of emotional problems your child may have. As children get older and focus on what they want for their lives, they develop better self-control.

192. Learn from Failures

It has probably become cliché to say that success comes from failure, but it is true. Life is never smooth sailing. We seldom get exactly what we want from life; most people must work for what they want. In the process of creating the life that you want for yourself, you will encounter many obstacles. The beauty of success is, you learn from your failures so as to get better and move in the direction you want to go. When you see your child stress over a failing grade, assure them it is part of the process. There is never anything wrong with failing. The problem is giving up when you fail, or not learning from the failure. Teach your child to discover the lesson they can learn in every failure, to keep failures in perspective, and to never take it personally.

193. Resourcefulness

Resourcefulness and creativity are two qualities which will go a long way in helping your child use their talents to create a meaningful life for themselves. When a child is resourceful, they tend to use every available tool to create something great for themselves. Children who are resourceful and creative may sell their used clothing online to make extra money, organize a fundraiser, or start a dog walking business. They think outside the box and have new ideas for moving their life forward. Resourceful children do not waste their time on distractions. They have goals to accomplish and often find things in their environment which will help them reach those goals. You nurture your child's resourcefulness by encouraging them in the positive things they want to do. Provide them with supplies if they want to build an arts and crafts project, and seek ways to nurture their creative genius.

194. Emotional Awareness

Anger is a very costly emotion! Teach your child as early as possible to gain control over their emotions. At school or in the workplace, an angry or unreasonable emotional outburst can be a huge setback for your child. Children who react unreasonably in school – such as hitting another child or verbally/physically abusing others – are either suspended or punished. You should also reprimand your child and punish accordingly for bad behavior. If you do not do it now, society will do it later through the juvenile system, or the prison system, by way of the courts. It may look like play now, but if these habits continue, they become criminal tendencies in adults. Teach your child to maintain emotional objectivity, to control themselves, and to be aware of others' feelings when dealing with people. Help them learn empathy and to care for others.

195. Potential

It is tempting to believe that some people are born smarter than others, or that some people have better luck than others. It is tempting to think that your lot is worse than someone else's. Truly, in a world of equal opportunities such as in the United States, you are what you believe. You are as good as you make yourself; you must strategically put in the effort and work hard. Potential equals hard work and nothing else. It is the willingness to wake up every day and give it your best shot; to apply hard work to your gifts and talents to achieve your goals and make a difference in your life. Teach your child the simple philosophy that nothing comes by birth but by work. Help your child to defeat the entitlement mentality and the erroneous belief that things will just magically happen without work.

196. Habits

The secret sauce of success is our habits. Habits are the things that we repeatedly do, day in and day out. Many people think that to wildly succeed they need to do a thousand and one things. Not necessarily. You only need to repeatedly do the one thing, the one habit, that will consistently move you towards your goal. So decide on that one habit, then become a person of discipline to ensure that you do it daily. Habit is a powerful principle to implement in your life as a parent, then teach it to your child. Encourage healthy habits at a very early age in the five essential domains of life – health, money, work, spirituality, and relationships. In each of these areas, encourage your child to develop one good habit that will propel them towards the goal of that domain. For instance, you want to start making sure that your child eats healthy, nutritious meals now so that it carries into their adulthood. This is a good, easy habit you can implement early.

197. Success Builds on Success

Teach your child to celebrate their accomplishments, and never to take anything they have achieved for granted. Sometimes, we tend to overlook and minimize our personal achievements. That is not healthy. Stop every so often and give yourself a pat on the back for a job well done. Success builds on success; the more you achieve, the better you feel that you *can* succeed. Have you noticed that people who feel appreciated always feel motivated to do better and increase their efforts? The more you succeed, the more you feel that you can do even better than your previous achievement. Be sure you make a big deal out of every experience that your child accomplishes. If they move their grades up, do well on the test, complete their homework neatly and on time, do the dishes on their initiative, take care of their little brother or sister, make sure you celebrate each of their accomplishments because it will motivate them to want to do more. Success builds on success.

198. Know Disciplinary Policies

Every school has a set of policies for disciplining students based on behavior. These disciplinary practices are based on the gravity of the conduct. Sometimes students will be suspended if they physically assault another student. Sometimes a teacher may rip a student's paper, or give the student zero on their work. It may also just be calling home to inform you of your child's behavior. Either way, as a parent, you must be aware of the various disciplinary policies that are in place for students, so that when it happens, it will not come as a surprise to you. Also, if the school disciplines your child for any reason, do not be in a rush to defend them. Find out what happened. Never assume that your child is innocent or rush to defend them until you hear the facts from all sides. Your child may not be as innocent as you believe.

199. Keep Rejection in Perspective

Teach your child about failure and rejection, to put these two truths into perspective, and to understand that they make life what it is. To succeed, you will hear the word "no;" you will receive rejections; you will fail a test; your grades and GPA may drop even though you have worked incredibly hard. It is never easy, but it is always worth it to keep rejection in perspective. Teach your child never to take failure and rejection personally, but instead to focus on the price, on the goal they desire to accomplish. A determined mind will always seek ways to go around a failure or rejection because the result is more important than the process. Give your child a vision for their future, and a reason why hard work is so worth it. Help them understand hard work may not always take them to their desired outcome, but it helps them develop the skill and character to make their future dreams come true.

200. Friendships

Provide opportunities for your child to attend community events. Community gatherings foster out-of-school friendships, thereby avoiding cliques and expanding their network of acquaintances. It will also expose their minds to other opportunities and broaden their horizons and thinking. Encourage them to make friends in other settings, thereby increasing the scope of their experience. Take your child to museums and children's events in your community. Also, look into the possibility of community college for children in the summer. There are many Arts and crafts summer programs offered for younger students at a discounted rate in some colleges. Include a blend of learning and fun events in your child's activities.

201. Mindset

We hear it said all the time: mindset is imperative to success. It is mindset which helps us decide to do something with our lives and face challenges. Never underestimate the power of the mind. To help your child develop a healthy mindset, you have to encourage them and teach them that they can achieve anything they set their minds to. You have to empower them. You have to make them feel they are enough, they have everything they need, and they have what it takes to succeed. A strong mindset comes from a place of determination, a belief that one can do what they set their mind to in their health, work, school, relationships, and spirituality. Children are not too young to begin thinking this way, and to order their lives along these lines. It takes a disciplined mindset to want to live an optimum life.

202. Listen to the Teacher

Listening is an essential skill that enhances student learning. Listening is the ability to pay attention in class and follow instruction. It is the primary way by which your child is going to learn. If your child does not listen in class and is distracted by other things, how are they going to acquire new information? Are they a good enough reader to comprehend the information on their own from the textbook? Are they a good enough reader to teach themselves the content? If not, then the only other way of learning the information is to pay attention in class and ensure that the information does not get away from him. Encourage your child each and every day as they leave home for school to be an active listener, to take notes of what is discussed, if possible, and being actively engaged in the learning process.

203. Ask Questions in Class

Generally speaking, you have to ask to get. That is the bottom line! The world is not waiting to serve all your needs, give you everything you want, and make your life more comfortable. You have to ASK! Asking is how you get what you need to fulfill your goals. It is the same in the classroom. You have to ask to clarify your understanding. Indeed, your child will learn a great deal simply by paying attention and listening to the teacher. However, if there are questions still lingering after the teacher has taught a lesson, encourage your child to raise their hand and ask for clarification before the teacher moves on to the next topic. If your child allows the teacher to move on to another concept without a full understanding of the previous one, they may miss crucial information and may not be able to pass the test later. This explains why many students struggle in school – they fail to ask questions. These strategies are vital to your child's learning.

204. Study, Read, or Research

The truth is that reading and studying can completely change the course of someone's life. That is what the love of reading did for me; it completely changed the course and trajectory of my life. Reading gave me many, many second chances. I have since learned that the most successful people in the world are avid readers. Reading expands your mind and gives you new ideas. The more you read, the more you know! So, provide several opportunities for your child to read. Encourage their reading skills. Not only will reading help them in the long run (in life), but it will also help them get through school a little easier. They will be able to take advanced classes, improve their chances of doing better on tests and quizzes, and do better on college reading assignments. I always say there is never anything wrong with reading! There are too many benefits, so raise a reader!

205. Mastering Mathematics

Math is one of those subjects in which one concept builds upon another. If your child has not learned or mastered the previous concept, it will be very hard for them to learn the subsequent ones. In other words, if your child has not mastered multiplication, it will be hard for them to know division because division is inverse multiplication. Make sure your child has foundational skills in math which will help them fully understand the major concepts. Math is an important part of STEM which is touted as necessary in the current job market. It is a gateway to science, which is one of the highest paying career fields. Encourage your child to pursue math and science subjects. Pay close attention to their performance in these areas, and ensure that they do not lag behind.

206. Extra Credit Work

Encourage your child to pursue extra credit work. Extra credit work supports your child in raising their overall GPA. It is not designed to make up for missing homework and shoddy work, but it can make the difference between a B+ and an A. So encourage your child to work for every extra credit point. Sometimes your child will ask for your help in obtaining supplies or sign a form as part of their extra credit work. Be generous with your support because it will help them gain a few more points that could move their grades up. Also, ask your child to discuss the possibility of getting extra credit work from their teacher. If they are serious about raising their grades, this may be a good way to show the teacher that they are committed to doing extra work.

207. Avoid Distractions

Distractions are the number one killer of dreams and potential in children (and adults). Your child's depth of knowledge on a particular subject will be severely impacted by distractions like text messages, browsing social media, watching videos, face-timing and talking on the phone instead of completing academic tasks. Many children get poor grades in school, not because they cannot understand the content, but because they are too distracted to master it. Distraction is a *major* cause for concern! As a parent, you must use every reasonable means to help your child develop good study habits.

208. Tests and Quizzes

Quizzes, weekly skills tests, benchmark tests, and state tests are an important part of your child's overall grade. They could also determine your child's admission into good colleges and universities. Encourage your child to take tests and quizzes seriously, and prepare for them properly. Fortunately, if your child has been consistent in studying, doing homework, and implementing many of the strategies we have discussed, then preparing for tests will just be a matter of reviewing the information. Remind them to review their notes and get a good night's sleep the night before a test.

209. Extra-Curricular Activities

Extra-curricular activities help your child find balance, and they give them a much-needed break from school work. Consider enrolling your child in an activity that they enjoy, either in-school clubs or outside school through sports, church or social events. As long as your child is balancing all they *want* to do with all they *have* to do, then school work and extra-curricular activities are coexisting very well, and can improve your child's grades. Also, encourage your child to take up leadership roles in the classroom by volunteering to help. This kind of support system builds a connection with the teacher, and could feed into academic performance.

210. Integrity

Getting good grades in school is important, but it is equally important to be a person of character and integrity. Teach your child never to cheat or copy someone else's work, always to do what is right, to honor their word, and keep their promises. Your child needs to persist and work hard, to never give up on themselves, and to never compare themselves with others. Teach your child to take full responsibility for their actions and decisions, to learn from their mistakes, and to never let anyone intimidate them or be bullied by their circumstances. Your child should ask for what they want, stand up for what they believe, help others and show empathy for others. And they need to be humble, but genuinely comfortable and confident in their own skin.

211. Recognize Your Child's Potential

Recognize that your child has the potential and God-given abilities to excel in school. Believe in your child, and help them believe in themselves. When you truly come to the realization that your child is born with unique gifts and talents, then you will begin to see the beauty in every aspect of your child and discover new ways to nurture those gifts to help them reach their academic goals. Listen to your child's emotional needs. Do not ignore or dismiss their feelings. Be that listening ear, that shoulder to lean on, that friend to confide in, and that person they can come to when their world is upside down.

212. Sacrifice

Being a parent is a one shot deal. You only get one chance to do it right. Just one. Give it your best, so that in your later years you will look at your child and say, "I gave him/her my all." This requires unwavering sacrifice during the years that your child depends on you for love, guidance, and safety. Congratulations to all the hard-working moms and dads out there who give it their best shot every single day, sometimes with very limited resources. My hat's off to you! I have shared these tips with you in good faith and an unshakeable belief in your child's ability to excel in school and life. Take what you need, and leave what you do not need, but let that belief drive your parenting decisions as well.

213. Abandon Inferiority

It has already emphasized that mindset is a critical component of success. A student's success in school is a direct reflection of how they think. If your child does not feel they are capable of success, they will not be able to succeed. Make it your intention to support your child's belief system, and encourage them to defeat inferiority in all its forms. When a child feels inferior, they do not believe they can accomplish anything. They do not feel worthy of success or anything good. Children with this mindset always feel someone else is better than they are, and usually, defer to other people's opinions. Help your child defeat any feelings of inferiority and inadequacy by encouraging them to be cognizant of their brilliance, and to see the beauty which lies within them. Always seek opportunities to point out the amazing things they do rather than criticize.

214. No Comparison(s)

Do not compare your child with their siblings or with other children. First of all, children do not like to be compared to others, and second, each child is special in their own way. They have their style of doing things which is unique to them. It may not make sense to you, but children have good reasons for feeling this way. It is true there will be times you want your child to do things differently, but continue to encourage them to stay focused on doing those activities that move their life forward. If you see your child doing something that you do not like, instead of saying to them, "Why can't you be more like your sister/brother?" give them support based on their unique issue. Address what concerns them on their terms and do not measure their actions against anyone else's actions, because everyone is different.

215. Move the Grades Up

Encourage your child to develop the goal of constantly wanting to move their grades up. Encourage them to never be satisfied with mediocre academic performance or low grades in school. Teach them to have a sense of confidence in their work and their ability. They should never be content with the way things are in their school work if they are failing. Give them the sense of self-worth and diligence they need to seek improvement and excellence continuously; it will be required in the marketplace after they graduate. Mediocrity in the workplace will be unacceptable. Employers want to see continuous growth and performance. They want to see that your child can solve problems and not let them escalate. Speak to your child often about the importance of working to move their grades up, even if it is a B grade. They must take strategic actions and implement habits toward the goal of moving their grades up.

216. Learn from Others

It is paramount for your child to know that it is okay to learn from and be inspired by others. It is okay to be inspired by others, as long as what you are imitating aligns with your goals and plans. Being inspired by others does not mean that you do not have your skills and sense of worth, it just means that you want to be a better person, improve yourself, and seek inspiration from others to do that. The only problem with being inspired by others is if your child feels a sense of inadequacy, or feel that someone else's approach is better than theirs. No one is better than anyone else. We all have our unique ways of seeing and doing things. So while you may admire what someone else is doing, it does not mean what you are doing is inadequate or insufficient. The goal is to continue to grow, improve, and seek ideas that move you in a positive direction.

217. Teach Good Manners

Increasingly, with the proliferation of technology, it looks like we're losing basic social mores of engagement and interaction. People are not connecting in person anymore. Most of our engagement is now online in the virtual world of technology. Let us not forget that we are still human beings who need to interact with each other at a human level. Children are beginning to forget the basic sense of propriety. Teach your child to be respectful to adults, to greet people when they walk into a room, and to respect themselves. Teach them to take responsibility for their actions, and to practice behaviors that present them in the best possible light. Teach them values and beliefs that nurture them in a positive way and give them a sense of wellbeing, along with the ability to interact well with others. Some children have a hard time adjusting to social situations, so your job is to continue to validate them and give them a sense of self-pride.

218. Not a Statistic

Teach your child to stand above the crowd. Help them learn to stay away from stereotypical behaviors that make them average and cause them to become a statistic. Teach them to stop manifesting negative behaviors that are typical of those in their age groups. For example, if your child is a boy, show them they do not need to be wearing their pants down low like other teenagers do. Remind your child that they do not need to spend all day on the social sites just because their friends do. Encourage your child to have a sense of judgment, and develop the character and courage to deviate from the norm. I am not saying that your child should isolate themselves. They should still have friends and hang out with them, but know when and where to draw the line. They do not have to do what their friends are doing just to fit in.

219. Raising a Productive Human

As parents, we tend to forget that how we raise our children impacts not just our immediate household, but the community and our world as a whole. You are raising a human being who will make contributions to the world. What kind of contributions will they make? Will they improve the community they live in or will they be a burden to it? What values are you passing on to your child that will make them productive citizens who enhance the world around them? Prisons are filled with criminals, and welfare rolls are filled with people collecting money from the government. These are all people's children, and somewhere along the line, something went wrong. Raise your children with the idea that you want them to give, not take, from the environment. Raise them to be their best so that they can serve their world, their country, and their community.

220. Use Uplifting Words

Many parents underestimate the power of their words and the impact those words have on their children. Heart-centered parenting requires that you intentionally use words that invoke positive feelings and outcomes in your child. As human beings, we bring to life the words that come out of our mouths and they will create a specific reality in your child's life. Ask yourself what impact you want your words to have, then use specific words that elicit feelings of completeness, joy, self-esteem, and confidence. One of your greatest joys as a parent will be raising children who have a great sense of themselves; who have a confident view of who they are; who trust their talents; who wake up every day with a beautiful feeling of what the world offers; who have a sense of purpose because they feel complete inside; and who feel loved. Use uplifting and empowering words to generate these positive feelings in your child.

221. Ask for Forgiveness

Teach your child to ask for forgiveness when they do something wrong. They need to "make right" what they have done wrong. As a parent, you want to raise a child who does not intentionally desire to hurt others or do wrong by others. You want to raise a child who shows empathy towards the real-life struggles of others. But, we are all human beings, and we all make mistakes. If your child makes a mistake or hurts someone's feelings, immediately have them apologize and ask for forgiveness. If you let this slide, they will feel their actions always deserve impunity, regardless of what they do. You are not teaching them proper character morals. If your child does something wrong to their siblings or does something against you, ask them to write a letter of apology. Most criminals who go to jail never feel remorseful for their actions. They have never been taught to apologize or ask for forgiveness. They do not understand empathy.

222. You Have What it Takes

One of your biggest jobs as a parent is to give your child a sense of pride in themselves, to make them see the beauty and power that lies within them. Help them understand that the source of their creation did not make any mistakes in them. They are fearfully and wonderfully made, with all the potential, power, and poise to create the outcome and goals which they want for their lives. Encourage your child to see they have what it takes, and that no matter how tough things get in life, they can always come through by the sheer power that lies within them. Teach your child to understand that by using their gifts, developing their skills, disciplining themselves, and forming healthy daily habits; they can rise to any challenge or situation that life hands them.

223. Be Authentic

We practically live in a copy-cat world; an era where social media and reality TV exposes the personal and very private aspects of people's lives with the goal of influencing minds. Such a world shapes our social mores and expectations, and people start to act and think like one another. There is so much peer pressure among age groups to fit in, and to look and sound like others in the group. Teach your child to stand out from the crowd. Teach them to be themselves and to be proud of themselves. Teach them to have their own sense of judgment, direction, and sense of self. It is okay to be entertained and to watch what others are doing, but by no measure should that ever define our morals and values. As a parent, you want to teach your child the right value system that aligns with your family beliefs.

224. Be an Overcomer

Being an overcomer gives your child the ability to face and tackle life challenges that are a part of living. School work will get tough; friendships will be strained; trust will be broken; parents will raise expectations of success; teachers will raise expectations; and counselors will demand more. Your child cannot buckle under the pressure of these expectations. They need to learn to overcome challenges, and not make excuses as to why they cannot do these things. You will have to impart upon them the reasons why they must handle these things with grace. Making excuses in life is a recipe for continually falling short of goals. Excuses are reasons why something cannot be done, as opposed to making opportunities to get them done. Help your child see positive outcomes in what they take on. Encourage their vision because it is that vision which will give them the *raison-d'etre* for pursuing actions instead of making excuses.

225. Intuition

I do not think we talk enough about the power of "intuition" or "hunch." Your intuition is that feeling that tugs at you to do something. As human beings, we all have it. Some people choose to listen to it and use it; some do not use it; others do not know they have it; others cannot hear it because they are immersed in the noise around them. Intuition is instrumental in making important decisions in one's personal life. It is important that your children focus and understand themselves, so they can listen to that still, small voice which tugs at them to make the right decisions in their lives. Distractions and outward stimulations hinder a child's ability to make sound choices that positively impact their decisions. You need to consistently encourage your child to focus on themselves so they can hear their inner voice which is like a compass, or roadmap, telling them where to go from one place in life to another.

226. Disappointments

There is no doubt that life will have its share of disappointments. There is no way around it. Friends will leave, you will fall short of your goals, you will need to work extremely hard, you will struggle, deals will fall through, you will hear the word "no" more times than you will hear the word "yes." Those are all acceptable parts of life. Teach your child to develop the ability to deal with disappointments, to face fear, failure, and frustration with courage. When disappointments happen in life, you either give up, or pick yourself up and find a different route. Many people have given up and, in the process, ruined their lives even more so than if they had dealt with the situation in the first place. As long as you are alive and breathing, you can always have a new beginning and brand new options. I say go for a new beginning and create new things, instead of moaning about what was!

227. Win, Do Not Whine

Nurture a winning spirit in your child. A winning spirit does not mean they should become so competitive and driven that it becomes an emotional issue which affects them if they do not get the results they desire. The opposite of a winning spirit is a whining spirit; always complaining about how things are not the way they should be. Raise a winner, not a whiner. Do this by consistently building your child's work ethic, encouraging them to give their best effort, teaching them to be purpose-driven, and instructing them to use their time to further their agenda. Avoid encouraging feelings of entitlement and privilege which cause children to believe they can have what they want without working for it. Sooner or later you will find that when they cannot have what they want, they will start whining and complaining. Nobody owes you anything, so stop whining.

228. Consistent Bedtime

Health and wellness advocates stress the importance of sleep, not only in adults but children as well. The brain needs sleep to rejuvenate itself and rest is necessary to think and perceive clearly. You can never underestimate the power of sleep. Children need sleep to be able to process information at school. A tired brain just cannot function properly. Mental acuity comes with enough sleep. So be sure to teach your child to protect their sleep by respecting early and consistent bedtimes. For younger children, they should be in bed at 8 pm and no later than 9 pm. For older children in high school with lots of homework, 11 pm should be the latest time they go to bed. Many students spend long hours on social media with friends, thus extending the time they need to complete their homework. This distraction can be costly. Teach your child to avoid distractions; do work first, then use relaxation time to connect with friends.

229. Study Space

Creative ideas flow naturally when one is in a quiet place free of interruptions. So many of our homes are noisy and loud, with people coming and going, loud music blasting, TV blaring. Family fun time makes life exciting, however, when this comes at the expense of student learning, it becomes a problem. Create a quiet environment when your child is trying to do their homework. Even better, provide them with a quiet space of their own where they can do their work uninterrupted. If your child does not have a room of their own, give them a specific space in the home which they can call their own. A study space helps them develop a good work ethic because they will take pride in using their space for creative explorations. Encourage them to respect the space and not use it to distract themselves but use it instead to produce good work.

230. Master Basic Skills in K-3

All learning starts in Kindergarten through third grade. Anything your child knows well in high school stems from what they learned in grades K-3. These grades are extremely critical in a child's life because this is when they learn foundational skills. If your child is in these grades, make sure they are mastering the basic foundation skills taught at these levels. Everything else they learn in later grades will build from these core competencies. For your child to read high-level AP subjects in high school, they must have mastered reading fundamentals in elementary school. For your child to fully understand Algebra, geometry, trigonometry, and calculus, they must have mastered addition, subtraction, multiplication, and division in elementary school. Concepts build upon concepts as they get older, so make sure if your child is struggling in elementary school, that you do all you can to assist them before they progress to higher grades.

231. Discipline

Our children are over-loaded with so much outward stimuli. There is so much going on in their surroundings, from friends to social apps, it is practically impossible sometimes for many of them to stay focused for an extended period. Mental discipline has become a very elusive concept; children find it hard to stay on task. Parents have resorted to all kinds of tactics to get their children to learn self-discipline, from taking away their phones to denying privileges. An important part of helping students build self-discipline is to teach them to take independent responsibility for their future. Let them know their future is in their hands and the choices they make today will either help or hinder them. Talk to them about having a vision for their future and working to accomplish all that is in their hearts to accomplish.

232. Trials and Tribulations

Teach your child that they will go through trials and tribulations and that there is nothing new about this; it is an essential part of life. Your child will become mature and tough as a result of the situations they will have to go through in life. If your child is struggling with anything, teach them to find the solution through research and reading how others have solved similar problems, and what suggestions they offer for addressing the issue. Plant this in their heads early on, and every time a challenging situation arises, use it as an opportunity to remind them it is a natural part of their existence. Teach them to take it in stride and seek a solution. Remember your struggles as a parent and how you handled those. How did you come through challenges you had in life? What kind of thinking helped you survive? Teach that thought process to your child.

233. Chief Influencer

As a parent, you are the chief influencer in your child's life. It is a tremendous responsibility to be able to influence someone's life, to cause them to shift their thinking and reposition their values and beliefs. To have such influence means that words, thoughts, and approach to things must be carefully orchestrated to achieve the desired result. Not only do you have to say it, but you must say it with tact. Many children do not listen to their parents; they argue with their parents and refuse to take their parents' opinions on things. As a parent, you just do not give up and say, "My child is not going to listen to me." You must say what is in your heart because it is in their best interest to know it. Sometimes we do not think they are listening, but trust me, they are; so you better be sure what you are saying makes sense.

234. People Skills

Teach your child to have people skills – the ability to relate to people and interact with them without feeling intimidated, inadequate, or shy. Having people skills come with a great sense of confidence which you have, hopefully, inculcated in your child. Encourage your child to boldly go up to people and ask for what they want. Teach them to be able to work with people of all ages, races, and walks of life. In the workplace, they will be expected to work with peers of different abilities. Some high schools now offer several group projects with the goal of getting students to interact with each other. Group interaction is the new marketplace reality; companies set up projects in teams and each team is expected to complete the project for the greater benefit of the business. The weakest link in the team will take the heat for all the members. Teach your child to have people skills so they will not be the weakest link on the team.

235. Willpower

Success requires willpower and developing a backbone. It is not easy to succeed in life, nor is it easy to succeed in school, but we all do it because we know what is ahead of us. The hard work is worth it for many. If you dream about a good life for your child, then you have to help them develop the willpower. You need to help them develop the ability to keep going even when a part of them wants to quit. If you want it badly enough, and if you do not want to short-change yourself in life, then you have no option except to put in the work that it takes. Will you always want to do the job? No. Will you always be enthusiastic about the work? No. But you must have the willpower to do it. When you feel frustrated and feel like you do not want any part of it anymore, take a short break and come back to it at a later date. Then you can look at it again from a fresh perspective.

236. Is School Boring?

Many students have said to me that they find school boring. Many times, this happens because they refuse to give the effort. Because they have not tried, their grades may be suffering as a result. Anybody who is struggling in any area of life will find it boring, too. If a child is struggling in school, it is natural for them to find it boring. It is true that some children find certain aspects of school boring because the curriculum may not be challenging enough for them. If your child tells you that they find school boring, ask them what their alternatives are. Ask what they can do to make school more exciting. Have an in-depth conversation with your child about their next step and how you can help them have a different view and mindset. Discuss the value of a good education and how they will benefit from it.

237. Leaders Follow First

To be a great leader, you have to consider the views of others. Teach your child that to develop leadership qualities; they need to know how to follow a leader. As your child learns to lead, they too will be leading effectively. Teach your child to follow the right kinds of people. They cannot just blindly follow people because they are popular and cool. Teach them to follow individuals who live exemplary lives and have principles that contribute to the greater good. The right kinds of people to follow will be parents and teachers who value their opinions. Therefore, be a good role model to your child and live an exemplary life. Teach them to have respect for authority; by doing this, they are living exemplary lives. Your child is likely leading right now in some capacity. Perhaps they are in a group project where their opinion counts. That is leadership.

238. Your Inheritance

Think about the people and great family members who have gone before you. Think about your ancestors and your grandparents, or that special someone who was very influential in your life but, unfortunately; they are no longer with you. What legacy did they leave for you? What lessons and experiences did they teach you? That is your inheritance. You have to leverage it and build on it. The way you honor and cherish your loved ones who have gone before you is to live your life in such a way that will them proud of you. They have left you with amazing memories, so use those memories to create a wonderful life for yourself. Your children will feel proud of you. Sadly, some people get so upset over losing someone special that they do the opposite. They feel stressed and depressed and ruin their lives. Think about the great world leaders and your family members who have been mistreated because of the values and principles they held. Honor their inheritance.

239. A Piece of Cake

I always love to talk about the cake metaphor! There are three kinds of people that life will hand a piece of cake to, based on your contribution to the universe. The first kind of person will be the person who has a seat at the table and eats their favorite piece of cake. They then take seconds, and they ask for different flavors. Their cake is decorated with chocolate syrup and a cherry on top. The second kind of person will eat their piece of cake, and the crumbs which are left over. They will scrape their plate for every little bit. The third kind of person will not eat a piece of cake, but will clean up after the big party. Which person are you? How do you raise your child so that they can enjoy the best of what life offers? All of us were born brilliant, but we limit ourselves and settle for the little things life offers. We do not put forth our best effort and therefore do not enjoy the fullness of life. Teach your child to go for the best that life offers!

240. Peace

The first step to teaching your child not to argue is by not arguing with them. When you argue with your child, you are teaching them how to argue. When you give instructions to your child, you have to follow with persuasive language, tone, and gestures that inform them of what they need to do or say. When children learn to argue, they talk back to you and have no respect for your opinion. This will make you miserable as a parent. You must immediately interrupt them and say, "do not talk back to your mother," or "respect your parents." Use this direct language consistently to let them know that it is not appropriate to argue with your parents. In the marketplace arguing, whining, and complaining will get your child nowhere. In fact, it can cause them to lose their job. Train your child to know that arguing and complaining are unacceptable.

241. Paint a Picture

As a parent, there is a picture in your mind's eye about how you see your child's future, how you wish for them to live their lives as adults. If you are like most parents, you probably want your child to live in a nice home, drive a nice car, go on vacation to remote destinations, and have enough extra money to give to charity and as gifts. Your vision for your child must be so clear that every cell in your body and every vein in our being can easily communicate it to them. Your vision must be so vivid that you do all in your power to raise your child with the right habits and skills to reach the place you dream about for them. Also, help them see what you see. When they understand your vision, they will want to take themselves there; they will assume responsibility for their lives and want to achieve that vision. This is why vision-boarding is so important for many people.

242. Self-Motivation and Self-Reliance

It is amazing how many people latch on to aids to get them going in life. They use Xanax, painkillers, marijuana, drugs – all for the purpose of staying high. Why do they feel the need for external stimuli to jolt them into action and enthusiasm? I have heard stories of many children who lack motivation for school, who do not want to give any effort, and who just want to do what they want to do. Is this your child? If so, then you have not painted a clear vision for them. You have not told them what is good and amazing about them. If you want your child to be self-motivated, you have to give them a reason why what they are doing will add joy and excitement to their lives. You have to tell them the amazing things that await them after they complete their schooling. If you want your child to be self-reliant, you have to tell them often that you believe in them, they are capable, and they have what it takes to excel.

243. Time for Everything

Encourage your child to understand that there is time and season for everything. There is time to play and time for work, time to be a kid and time to be an adult. In due season, they will achieve the milestone of each time. There is no reason they should ever feel they need to be doing something else and set aside the things they should be doing. Many children would rather stay on the phone than do their school work. Some would rather go out partying and try to act older before it's their time. Remind your child that it is such a beautiful season to be a child, and encourage them to enjoy every minute of that season; to stay focused on their lives and nourish every aspect of who they are, to be what they dream. Discourage them from friends who take their attention away from doing the things that will move their lives forward.

244. Focus, Commitment & Discipline

These are the three words which move every important person toward achieving their dreams. If you want your child to succeed in school, they have to learn and implement these principles in their lives. Many erroneously believe that these principles make life difficult and painful. That may be true in some instances, but they bring you success, also, in every area of life that you choose. Something has got to give to be the person that you dream of becoming. If you want to be a healthier person, you have to stay focused, committed and disciplined in doing the things that you need to do to be healthy. If you want your child to be successful, you must always remind them to pursue their school work with focus, discipline, and commitment. Teach them to stay committed to their vision by implementing specific habits that move them in the direction they wish to go.

245. Gossip

Do not gossip, judge, or put down other people in front of your child. If you do this, what message are you sending them? The only thing this teaches your child is to lose trust in people, have reservations about people, be insecure about their environment, and to lose faith in others. If you must gossip about someone, take the conversation out of the presence of your child. Ironically, gossiping speaks louder about who you are as a person, as opposed to who the person is that is the subject of your gossip. Some parents go so far as to gossip about teachers and school administrators at the school their children attend. How do you expect your child to have respect for authority when you do this? Let your child discover a person's nature for themselves. Let them develop their own relationships with people. In the natural course of those relationships, they will decide how to interact with individuals in a way that is positive.

246. Set Personal Goals

Goals are what move us from one point to another in life. Goals are essential for achieving what you desire. Setting goals does not mean that you have to be dogmatic about meeting them. It does not mean that you have to give up living to achieve your dreams. The idea is to enjoy the journey as you work towards your goal. In other words, the destination is great, but the journey is even more beautiful. So enjoy the journey! Do not get so hung up on reaching your dream that you get frustrated. Goals give you a framework to rise to your next level. Encourage your child to set goals, such as moving their grades up in math, or English. Help them to set health goals, like eating more fruits and vegetables. Set a personal goal, and then take action by doing something small each day to reach your goals.

247. Action

The one word that changes everything in a person's life is "action." Without action, nothing gets done. We all know the famous slogan by Nike, *"just do it."* That is what it comes down to; getting stuff done by taking action. Teach your child to be a doer, to not be lazy. To be successful in school, you must study. To be healthier, you need to exercise, so get out there and get your exercise done! If you do not want to take action, then you will not get much done. As a result, you may struggle in many areas of life. One way to help your child develop the stamina to take action is to assign household chores and tasks. Have them assist you in your home business or while you prepare a family meal. Give your child something to do when possible and see that they complete it. You are not punishing them; you are building their resiliency in being action-oriented.

248. Your Circle of Friends

Our relationships in life make a tremendous difference in our emotional wellbeing. The friends your child surrounds themselves with will make a significant difference in their life. Teach your child to find and make friends with peers whose vision aligns with their own. When you make friends with someone who is not interested in school, you will become disinterested in school. If you make friends with someone who has goals and a vision for their life, you will envision incredible dreams for your life. Talk to your child about their friends. If you suspect your child has an unhealthy friendship, have a sit down conversation with them and point out how that relationship will negatively impact their future. As your child grows older, they will discover that the right relationships will help them get ahead in life

249. 24-Hour Days

We all have 24 hours in our day., but some people produce a lot more with their 24 hours than others. Why is that? It is because they are highly productive; they use their time wisely, and they want to account for their hours. Teach your child effective time management and how to use their day productively. Teach that every minute of their 24-hour day is valuable and should be used for activities that move their lives forward. Encourage your child to always have a to-do list and check things off that list as the day goes on. A to-do list means that each day your child will write down a list of items they wish to accomplish for that day, and then they check the items off once they are complete. This is a great activity that will keep them focused on achieving more of the goals they want to accomplish!

250. Siblings

Encourage siblings to build each other up. It is essential that your children see each other as the people they can lean on in times of difficulty. The world out there is cruel; everybody is going about their business, and they have their own issues to worry about. They do not have time to worry about what is happening in your family and what kind of challenges you may be going through. There are also people out there who will set out to hurt you, and they will find every means to do it. Trust me when I say, nobody can help fight your battles better than a member of your family. That is why you must teach your children to stick together as a family. You need to motivate them to join in the battle against outside forces, and not against each other. Teach your children to spur each other on, to not be envious or compete with each other.

251. The 60-Minute Rule

Another vital strategy in helping your child use their time wisely is the 60-minute rule. This rule is simple: your child is to focus on a particular task or activity for 60 minutes. During those 60 minutes, they must turn off all distractions and focus entirely on the task at hand. There are variations of this rule. You may do 120 minutes, 30 minutes, 45 minutes, or however many are needed to complete a task. This principle will make a difference in getting your child to focus on the work at hand and in their personal lives as they get older. Many adults struggle with completing goals and projects because they are not dedicated enough to invest the time it takes to complete it. If you start to groom your child early on to allocate a specified amount of time toward completing their work, you are teaching them a skill that will add tremendous value to their lives.

252. Create, Do Not React

Again, the entertainment value of technology is such that people find excitement in looking at what is happening in other people's lives and the world at large. Reality TV has ushered in a trend where voyeurism is considered entertainment. From this vantage point, they are "reacting" to the world around them without offering anything of their own. YouTube videos are another trend, with thousands and thousands of fans following people they do not know. Always be encouraging your child to be the kind of person who "creates" stuff of their own and does not just "react" to what others do. It is true that many of us find inspiration by watching what others do; however, we have to be watching for the purpose of making our contributions. Teach your children to be creators more than consumers.

253. Act the First Time

When you give your child instructions to do something, make sure they do it the first time they are asked. They cannot do it when it is convenient for them, or at a later date. They have to do it when you ask them. If they fail to do it, remind them that you instructed them to do something, and you would like it to be done immediately. Obedience is a habit which will be instrumental to your child's success as they get older. Procrastination is the biggest culprit in preventing adults from reaching goals. Also, not being teachable is another culprit. When you allow your child to get away with not doing a task when it is assigned, they may develop the habit of procrastinating or not being teachable by mentors. You cannot succeed in life and business if you are not teachable and if you procrastinate.

254. Do It for You!

One of your biggest challenges as a parent will be to teach your child to take ownership of their work and their life. Many children tend to think that they are doing their schoolwork and household chores for their parents, to please them. As a fellow parent, I know you require these things to help your child be a successful and productive adult who can take care of themselves independently. While it is true your tone or approach may be harsh sometimes; the idea is to get your children to realize you are doing it for them, and they are doing it for themselves – not for you! Encourage them to dedicate themselves to their chores, their school work, and their future. Encourage them to be their number one fan and cheerleader. Teach them to take ownership of their work and have their best interest at heart, because nobody will fight for them more than they can fight for themselves.

255. Older siblings

Teach your older children to be role models to their younger siblings. Being older is a privilege, and it is an honor to have a younger person look up to you as a result of your years of experience. It is a position which must not be taken lightly. An older sibling is an influential person who is in charge of the wellbeing of younger siblings. Being influential does not mean exercising unreasonable authority at will. It means caring for siblings and ensuring they are emotionally and physically fine. Assign your older child responsibility for their younger siblings by encouraging them to read with them, help them with homework such as math, teach them valuable life skills, and teach them to make good decisions. This is an excellent way to nurture love and closeness between your children and it gives you some time to focus on other things as a parent.

256. Know Your Child

To get the most out of your child, you must be aware of their personality. It is interesting how some parents do not know their children's character or what they are capable of doing. This may be because parents bring their preconceived notions and truths to the parenting relationship. They assume the things they did as children, or they witnessed happen to other children growing up, or their parents did to them, may also be their children's experience. This preconception has a downside; you are trying to align your child with a reality which is not their own, and you expect them to make decisions and judgments based on that reality. Take time to study your child, know who they are, know their strengths and weaknesses, and groom them based on those truths. Address their weaknesses without condemning them, but instead show them alternative options. Praise their strengths and teach them to do more of what works.

257. Trapped in Busyness

Recently, I was in a conversation with a group of parents. We were discussing why many children struggle in school and never meet their academic goals. One parent suggested the main reason is that parents are caught up in their agenda. Parents are very busy with their lives, working and doing various things during the day, and do not have time to invest in their children. Another parent noted that many people are distracted and spend a lot of their time online and on social media when they could be spending that time focused on helping their children. Whatever the reason, children are often left on their own without supervision. And, during their unsupervised time, they do everything except schoolwork. With this in mind, try not to get caught up in your agenda. It is true that you have a lot of things to do as a parent to meet the needs of your child, but please also remember it is all fruitless if you lose your child in the process.

258. Recognition

Everybody loves praise and recognition. Always try to catch the good in your child. Something as small as a 'thank you' will make them feel appreciated. Try to applaud them for completing chores around the house, for excellence in working, and for being diligent in their tasks. These are skills and attitudes that will get them recognized and promoted in the workplace, earn raises, and receive awards. It will cause them to grow their businesses and care for their marriages. It is not about the task itself; it is their attitude towards the job that counts. It is about efficiency when completing a task, diligence in completing the work, and accepting the challenge to finish the job in the first place. These are the things you want to reward and recognize. Do not acknowledge work that is sloppy or done with a poor mindset. Teach your child to change their attitude through recognizing their obedience.

259. Family Honor

Many parents make demands on their children to uphold their family honor or prove something to the world. They do not want their child to embarrass them as parents, so they make unreasonable decisions that place enormous pressure on their children. The impact of this can sometimes be devastating, with children feeling they have to make their parents happy and uphold the family name. It is important to hold our children to high expectations, but the motive should not apply pressure to your child. It must be in their best interest, not something for you or your family's best interest. As a parent, you always want to encourage your child to be the best they can be, to pursue personal development, and to focus on activities that prepare them for a successful future. None of these things have to do with you or your family's honor; they have to do with choices which are in your child's best interest.

260. A Bright Future

As a parent, you are supposed to bestow blessings, not curses, on your child. The history of generational poverty must stop with you. See your child as the successful person they will eventually become. Do you believe that your child is intelligent and has the power to experience a prosperous future? Do you believe that your child can be wealthy? Wealth is not just for a special few who have been designated to be rich; it is a mindset. If you believe your child is capable of success, then you must position them to do activities which will help them grow and be successful. Many parents have low self-esteem themselves and do not believe they are good enough to succeed beyond their current situation. They pass on this limited thinking through decisions regarding their children. Hold your child to higher standards and expectations and give them a bright future.

261. Financial Burden

The burden of financial lack is huge for many families. If you are one of those families, there are several questions you will have to ask yourself. Do you want your child to struggle financially like you have? Do you want your child to worry and stress over not having enough money like you have? Do you want your child to have a burden of debt? Do you want your child to live paycheck to paycheck? Do you want your child to run out of money before the end of the month? Do you want your child to live in a small, cramped apartment? Do you want your child not to be able to pay their rent or mortgage? Do you want your child to work several odd jobs just to make ends meet? I am sure, like most parents, your answer to these questions is an adamant "no." Teach your child to set financial goals.

262. Financial Freedom

Like most parents, I have no doubt you want your child to enjoy ultimate financial freedom in every area of their lives. With a competitive global market, a struggling economy, and the housing market the way it is today, enjoying financial freedom is a real concern. It will take a deliberate strategy to position your children in careers and fields that will afford them the lifestyle of freedom. As a parent, you have the responsibility and an obligation to ensure that you are positioning your child for financial success and success in every area of their lives. Right now, many parents do not even spend enough time with their children because they have to work round the clock to take care of the bills. Since you have the experience of financial struggle, you have a moral obligation to teach your children not to go down the same route as you. Tell them the truth about real life and help them set goals to be financially free.

263. Poverty Mindsets

As a parent, you must rid yourself of the poverty mindset and teach your child to do the same. Do not blame your lack of knowledge about money on your parents. At some point as adults, we need to come into a place of consciousness that enables us to make decisions apart from the ones we were raised with. When you have high expectations for yourself and want different outcomes for your life, you'll reject beliefs that no longer serve youj. You are in control of what you want to pass down to your children. My hope is that you do not want to pass down the curse of poverty that has been passed down from generation to generation in your family. Seek several opportunities to equip yourself with the skill of handling, managing and making money. Read books on the subject, seek mentors and coaches, listen to audio programs. Gain knowledge on this, then teach it to your children; rescue your family from the poverty mindset.

264. Spending

Your child will model your spending habits. If you are one who indulges in excess spending, they will copy the same behavior; they will feel entitled to excess belongings just to satisfy their shopping craving. On the other hand, if you are frugal, they will also think twice about spending money. There is a clear difference between wants and needs. Teach your child to ask a question before every purchase, "Do I need this, or do I just want it?" Most of your child's expenses should be needs, not wants. It is okay to occasionally treat your child, or reward them for something they did, by giving them something they want. But just giving them something because they want it, and you have the money, is not a good way to approach spending; it only nurtures greed, materialism, and selfishness.

265. Giving

Teach your child not only about spending, but about giving as well. Part of the reason you want your child to do well is so they can have extra money to give back. They can give back to the church through offering and tithing, they can donate to charity, they can help others who are struggling and need some financial help, they can give as gifts to celebrate the successes of others. Find ways to help your children earn money around the house, then teach them how to not only spend wisely but to give to others as well. Giving is a big part of receiving; it is a great feeling to know you have made someone else's life just a little better through your ability to give financially.

266. Closeness

No matter how much money you make as a parent, your child will thirst for one thing from you – closeness. Bonding. It does not matter if you are rich or poor. Your child lives for your love and attention. There is a saying that "children need your presence, not your presents." This is such an accurate statement. Seek every opportunity to bond with your child. Go outside and play catch, go to the park and swing, go shopping together, or visit friends and family members. Play board games, dance together, text/call each other during the day to check up on each other or watch movies together. There are so many things to do! Above all, have respect for each other. You can be your child's parent, but you can also be their friend. Always try to bond with your child; these are the memories they will remember as they get older and have families of their own.

267. Be Resilient

As a parent, you have likely experienced your share of challenges and difficulties in life. Your child is watching how you handle crisis situations. They draw their strength from you. No matter how hard it gets, never allow your family to fall apart or be in jeopardy. Never expose your child to a dangerous situation out of desperation. We have heard horrific stories of how some parents practically expose their children to danger just to make a buck. No matter how dire your situation may be, hold your head up high and try to find a solution to your problem. No problem lasts forever. If you have to get three jobs just to make ends meet, do it. Do what you need to do to keep your child safe and stable at all times and never let your life fall apart. Be a resilient parent who can handle their business and still give their children love, attention, and self-esteem.

268. Role-Model

Be your child's number one role model. Be the kind of parent whose child values their opinion; whose child asks their opinion first before seeking the opinion of others. To earn this level of trust, you must be present for your child, guide and teach them yourself (from an early age). Live an exemplary life. You cannot live a life as an alcoholic, going out partying, screaming all the time, having no job and being lazy, and expect to be your child's role model. They will have no respect for you. Teach your child valuable life lessons by living those lessons yourself. Be hardworking, do not make excuses, be healthy, pray, do not be wayward, be disciplined, and love your family. These are the things that your child will copy from you. These are the things that make you a better role model than anyone else out there.

269. Exercise and Fitness

Make fitness, health, and wellness an integral part of your family lifestyle. Seek to keep yourself and your children healthy through what you eat and how you exercise. There is so much conversation around the importance of staying healthy, but many people do not do it – do not be that kind of parent. Always try to prepare home cooked meals for your children as opposed to eating out all the time. Not only is this a healthier alternative, but it also helps you save money. In your home cooked meals, opt for more fruits and vegetables. Stay away from fats and sugars. Teach your children about the adverse effects of junk food. Go out with your child to the park and take a walk, encourage them to go out to the back yard and play. Get into a dance contest with your children and make fitness a fun family event.

270. Your Vision

Being a parent does not mean you lose sight of your vision. What dreams do you have for your life? How did you envision your life before you became a parent? Are you living that dream? Are there things you want to accomplish for yourself and your future? Someday your children will grow up and leave home, and you will find the reality of your life staring back at you. Do not wait until then to start wondering what to do. Do not wait until boredom and confusion set in before trying to decide what to do with your life (at that point you will be acting out of desperation). Start now! Think about your future and think about what you desire in your heart and take the first step towards creating that reality for yourself. If you have to go back and take a community college class, do it. If you need coaching, do it. If you need to read and learn more about it, then do it. Start now and work towards something big.

271. Your Passion

Each person on earth has a unique mission to accomplish. That mission is called your passion. What do you love? What is your heart tugging at you to do? Each day, try to find quiet time to listen to that small voice which tells you what is exciting. Once you know what it is, do not ignore it. Do not let fear and doubt creep in to steal your passion. Do not let anything intimidate you from taking the first step toward making that passion come to life. Boldly take on the challenge of birthing your passion. Have courage in doing so, knowing your heart does not lie. Take a minute from reading this and ask yourself, "What do I want?" What is your heart telling you? What difference do you want to make in this world? What contribution can you make either to the community or your family? What are you passionate about? How can you use your time to pursue that passion?

272. Your Sense of Self

As a parent, it is essential to have a sense of self. To be the best parent you can be, you must be the best version of yourself. Think about how to improve yourself and grow; think about what you have to do to be spiritually, mentally, physically, and emotionally healthy. Avoid people and things that add stress to your life, because stress robs you of control. You are never too old to develop your sense of completeness and belief in the beauty of who you are. Cherish every moment and seek to live your best life by pursuing activities that add a sparkle to your day. Discover the best ways you can live out loud in every area of your life, from health to spirituality, work to relationships. Make the best of these areas as you get older; they will help you develop a greater sense of fulfillment in yourself. Remember that fulfillment is key!

273. Empty Nest

Sooner or later, your children will grow up and leave your home. What plans do you have for your life when that happens? Many parents wait until their children leave home before they start thinking about what to do with their lives. As they adjust to the new norm, they are at a loss about what to do, and that is when boredom sets in. Many parents fail to plan their future and then wonder what is next for them, as health challenges creep in. It is essential to develop a complete life plan and think about how you will use your time wisely as your children age. Some empty nesters like to travel and enjoy vacations; others plant a garden; some volunteer; others spend time entertaining friends and family. Whatever you decide to do, it should not be at the spur-of-the-moment. You need to take some time today to think about it and decide how your life will look in the future so that it brings you fulfillment.

274. Passing on Beliefs

Beliefs are an instrumental part of your parenting. Your belief system plays a tremendous role in influencing your child's belief system. If you have low self-esteem, do not let that pass on to your child; do not treat them as if they have low self-esteem, too. Even if your child struggles in school, do not let their struggles define who they are and conclude that they are not good enough. You must have a strong sense of confidence and belief in your child, know that they are capable of excelling, and take concrete steps at home to see the results of your expectations for your child. If you feel you lack belief and confidence in yourself, read motivational books. Also, ask yourself what is causing these limiting beliefs you have and take steps to correct your thinking so you can have two legs to stand on when teaching your child to have faith and confidence in themselves. Do not let limiting beliefs prevent you from reaching your goals!

275. Your Childhood

How you perceive your childhood will make a huge difference in how you raise your children. As a parent, you only know what your parents taught you, but you do not know what you do not know. You can only teach your children what you know. You can also intentionally make a decision to change some of your ideas about raising children. Perhaps your parents did some things which you liked or did not like. Take a moment to evaluate your childhood and reflect on how you felt growing up. Are there things you want to change? Are there things you want to keep? Try not to pass on things from your childhood that you think will hurt your child. Whatever you do, remember that your child's emotional and physical safety come first; take their best interest to heart.

276. Your Experiences

Your experiences in life count for something; do not dismiss or minimize the things you have experienced. Tell your child about the experiences you have had in your life and how those experiences have shaped you. Children, especially teenagers, sometimes forget their parents had a life before they had children, and they do not listen as their parents teach them what they know. Keep talking, because it is essential to guide your child toward making smart decisions based on your experiences. When you see your child making a wrong decision, use your experience to show them what you did in similar situations and how you experienced setbacks. Tell them stories about the experiences of other people and the choices they made as well. Life experiences are what drive our current decisions, so use yours to shape your parenting practices.

277. Your Investment Habits

Whatever your source of income, it is important to invest in your child's educational future. Teach your child about investment practices by saving and investing yourself. Many parents have the mentality that "one life to live" so spend what you have; they have no sense of putting money away to support their children's future. Instead, they spend their money on daily frivolities, buying little things here and there. You need to have a bigger vision for your child's life; plan accordingly to ensure that your child has the future you both dream. No matter how much money you make, invest some each month in your child's successful future. Not only are you teaching them good money habits, but you are also sending the message that their future and their education is important to you. Investing in your child's future is a matter of principle which speaks highly about you and your values.

278. Nutrition

I have talked several times about health in this anthology, but it bears repeating because of how important it is. The gateway to radiant health is proper nutrition. As many times as this has been reiterated many people tend to take it for granted and ignore it altogether. Diet is imperative because it lays the foundation for either good health or future health problems in your child. Heart disease and stroke, for example, are linked to nutrition. Those who have these conditions were once children who were not taught to take proper care of their health to avoid these diseases. Teach your child to make healthy choices, to limit sugar intake, and avoid fatty foods which clog the arteries. Ask your children's doctor about adding supplements to their diet. You have to consciously make wise choices for your child to give them the best shot at a long, healthy, vibrant, and boisterous life.

279. Prayer Avails Much

Pray *for* your children and *with* your children. Take them to church to give them a spiritual foundation. Such a foundation is necessary to help them live life in perspective and to find meaning in all they do. Pray about your children's future, for their salvation, and for their future spouse. Pray that your children have a great relationship with God and that they apply godly principles to their daily lives. Pray for a hedge of protection over their lives that they will be safe, and they will make informed choices. Pray that your children are not harmed and live happy lives as children/adults. Pray for God to give you the wisdom to raise them wisely and to make sound decisions which move them in the right direction. Pray He gives you the tools you need to support your children in every area of their lives.

280. Your Friendships

Being a parent does not mean that you cannot have friends of your own, or that your life totally revolves around your children. Have a good circle of friends which you can totally fall back on and share your life struggles. Relationships add so much meaning to your life and bring fulfillment. Keep a close group of friends who add meaning and value to your life; friends (or even family members) who can intervene to support your children when you need their help. Seek friends and family members who have your best interest at heart and who love you for who you are. Very often, parents are so entrenched with their children that they forget to live their lives. Take some time to go out and celebrate with your friends. Go out to eat, to a movie, to visit each other in your homes, and just find opportunities where you can take some time off from family responsibilities and bond with your friends. You will be a better parent for it.

281. Enjoy Inner Peace

Find peace within your soul. Take a little time to connect with yourself. It could be just a few minutes a day in the morning before the children wake up. Read an affirmation, say a prayer, center yourself, and feel the love and passion that your spirit generates. Pull back from the noisy world and celebrate your personal strength. Find inner peace and serenity; these two are like anchors which keep you grounded while lifting the burden of all you have to accomplish each and every day as a parent. Inner peace will give you the clarity and calm you need to handle your day. You will make better decisions as a parent, and you will guide your child from a place of love, not uncertainty. You will develop a better relationship with your child when you come to terms with who you are.

282. Respect Your Spouse

Show respect for your spouse in front of your children. Do not belittle, intimidate, or disrespect your partner in their presence. If you do, you are teaching them to do the same, not just to your spouse, but other people as well. Do not teach them to communicate this way. I have seen children be very rude to a parent because the other parent disrespects their spouse. Do not gossip about your spouse to your children. When you do this, you poison their relationship. Allow your child to base their relationship on their interaction with their parent and not on what you say or think about your spouse. Negative influence coming from you does not help your child; it only hurts them. Do not teach them to be bitter or to have a poor opinion of someone else. Handle yourself like a grown up, and do not get your children involved in your personal issues.

283. Your Fears

Every day I see adults who doubt themselves, who are intimidated by their environment, who are uncertain about their ability to handle specific issues, who are unsure of themselves and doubt that they can accomplish a particular goal. I see adults every day who do not have a strong sense of self, who are emotional and take things personally, who are quick to anger. I see adults who suffer a deep lack of self-esteem because they do not feel competent enough or educated enough. I see adults who do not know the first thing about being successful in business, or who do not know how the education system works. Because of this complete lack of knowledge and sense of self, they do not feel competent in supporting their children. They see their children as an extension of themselves and doubt that they can ever succeed. Do not pass on your limiting beliefs to your children. Your only job is to have high expectations for them, whether you believe they can do it or not.

284. Unconditional Love

Unconditional love should probably have been the first point discussed in this book. If you cannot love your child unconditionally, then anything you do as a parent will be for nothing. None of us are perfect; we all have our shortcomings, we all make mistakes. However, we can give our deliberate, intentional best as far as raising our child is concerned. Your divine mandate, the reason why God gave you this child, is to provide them your best. You are to provide for them and love them with all that you have in your being. Encouragement is the easiest way to get the best from your child; look for opportunities where they have done great things, and praise them. Be on the alert all the time as far as your children are concerned. Be ready to intervene immediately to address any situation that they may be experiencing.

285. Persist

No one said parenting would be easy, but it will be worth it. All your years of hard work and dedication will come to pass, and you will see the fruits of your labor. Parenting is like a season. First, you plant the seeds, then you watch them grow, and then you harvest the fruits. Enjoy the journey. Plant seeds by teaching your child healthy habits and good values from a very early age. Teach them the values and principles of success they need to apply in their daily lives so they can reach their goals. When you invest time and effort toward planting seeds, you are sure to reap a bountiful harvest. Your parenting journey will be difficult, bumpy and frustrating at times, but stay the course. Be patient and look at the big picture – you are raising high achievers who contribute to the world in a positive way and who can independently take care of themselves.

286. Become Debt-Free

We have talked about how you have to be a good role model for your child. One of the ways of doing this is to teach your child to be debt-free by being debt-free yourself. The burden of debt is a tremendous problem for many people. This is mainly the result of either living above your means or lacking the finances for your day-to-day living expenses. Debt is an emotional burden. Nobody thinks it is funny to have creditors calling your home repeatedly to collect on a debt. Remember, it is not how much money you make, but how much you keep. Your priority is to get out of debt, and your second priority is to begin saving money. Teach your children not to spend money they do not have, and to save what they do have. Teach them to pay attention to the things they spend their money on. It has to be needed, not wanted.

287. Change Starts Within

Understand that change starts from within. To be a better parent, you have to look at yourself in the mirror and ask, "Are there things about me that I need to change to be the best person for my children? Are there habits I have which I do not want my children to copy?" We have all seen parents who fall apart emotionally because they cannot handle tough situations in life. The foster care system is crowded with children whose parents have fallen apart. It is true that not all of these situations are self-imposed, but the majority are. While you may not consider yourself one of such parents, at some level we all have to examine ourselves and make personal changes where needed so we can be the best. As a parent who is raising a human being, you have to dedicate yourself to personal excellence by seeking to improve every day.

288. Work and Play

Do not sacrifice your children for your life and your dreams. Do not be so driven that you lose connection with your children. The reason you work is to provide for your children, but what good is work if you lose your child in the process? If all you do is work and you do not create opportunities to speak with them or spend time with them, your children will resent you, and what you do, and they will go in the complete opposite direction. Many busy parents have lost their children to the streets because they are always away from the home. I have been witness to many children who have experienced rejection and isolation because their parents never had time for them. They resorted to friends who gave them the love and attention they desired. Working hard can be a high price to pay. Create a balanced life which involves work *and* time with children. That is the beauty of life. You can have it all – love, work, health, and spirituality. You do not need to sacrifice one for the other.

289. Gratitude

No matter how bad you think your situation is, there is someone else who is worse off than you. Show gratitude for your life. Always be living in a state of gratefulness. When you are grateful for the little, you will receive more. Be grateful that your children are healthy, that you are healthy, that you can provide for your children, and that they are doing well in school. Be grateful that you have the opportunity to spend time with your child, for your loving relationships, and for people who support you. There are so many things to be grateful for in life which only you know about. Take some time to breathe and be grateful for where you are in your life. Live in gratitude every day and as you are grateful for the little things, you will find big things to be grateful for, too!

290. Competitiveness

Competition is not always a bad thing, but, among students, it is becoming a lost art. Many children just do not care about it. Competition is healthy because it not only measures your performance against the performance of others, but it positions you for opportunities which you could lose if you are not able to compete with what others are bringing to the table. We are talking about an increasingly competitive market. Many students are highly skilled and are positioned for good careers and jobs that will influence their future lifestyle. Your child has to match that level of competition to position themselves, too, and not get left out. They have to develop the skills, talents, and attributes that will enable them to have the results to match other talents in the marketplace. Encourage your child to be ready for a very competitive world where they will be expected to outperform other students to get into the college of their dreams and get a good career.

291. Self-Reliance

Focus is a major problem for many children – for many adults, too. The world around us is so busy; it takes a very dedicated person to stay focused on the things they need to accomplish. There are so many expectations of what we need to be doing; for children especially, they can get confused about what is expected of them. You want to consistently encourage your child to stay focused on themselves, to see the beauty that lies within them, and to realize they are complete in themselves. The most efficient way to do this is to create a home environment which gives your child high self-esteem. It is also important to have a relationship with your child that nurtures their personality and identity. When your child feels accepted and approved by you, they will not feel a need to seek outside approval. You also want to give them a vision for their lives and give them responsibility for their future. If they can clearly see a bright future for themselves, they will want to do what it takes to get there.

292. (Un)Popularity

Teach your child they do not need to be popular. Teenagers think they must be popular to be accepted among their peers. Let your child know they do not need to be accepted by anyone except themselves. It is essential they have a healthy sense of self and know they do not need anyone else to make them feel whole. How you make them feel at home is important, too. It is not enough to tell them they are special; you must make them feel loved by having a relationship which empowers them. Look for opportunities to praise them and recognize their efforts for the little things they do. When your child has a complete sense of self, the need to be popular and stand out among their friends will go away– and people will like them for who they are!

293. Leadership Skills

Teach your child leadership skills. Leadership requires that your child takes the initiative for ideas and execution. It requires your child to complete tasks that have been assigned to them when they are assigned to them. Sometimes, at home, you will assign your child certain chores, and they will either not do them, or do them when it is convenient for them. You want to have a conversation with your child about this. Assign specific chores to them which they are required to complete with automaticity. They should not need to be reminded to perform these tasks; they should take the lead in doing them as part of their living arrangement. Your child should also take the lead to ask for what they want from the people around them. Teach them to interact with others appropriately. All of these leadership qualities will help develop skills which will empower them for projects in the 21st-century workplace.

294. Creativity

Nurture your child's creative genius; encourage creativity. Many children spend hours watching videos of others online. It has become a habit, and they do not realize how it affects them. Not only is it distracting, but it causes children to feel what others have to say is more important than what they have to offer. Encourage your child to think about creating ideas of their own. Encourage them to nurture their gifts and talents. What is your child good in? What new skills can they acquire over the summer months that will empower them to use their time wisely? Does your child love computer coding, crocheting, or singing? Do they enjoy dancing, the business world, or any sports? Take time to discover what your child loves to do outside of school, then provide them with numerous opportunities to practice their craft. Invest in it and pay for programs if necessary.

295. Listen, Do Not Judge

One time I was speaking at a seminar, and I asked teenagers what is the biggest problem they have with their parents. Almost unanimously, the students said their parents do not listen. Now you know—they feel you do not listen! Make a conscious effort to hear your child when they are speaking to you. Look at them; make them feel heard. Do not judge them and conclude that they should be doing something a certain way instead of doing it their way. Allow them to explain themselves and give their point of view. You may see a motive for their actions which will make complete sense to you after all. Listen with an open mind and an open heart. Do not intervene to offer your opinion until you are asked. Do not judge or conclude that your child has or has not done something unless you have heard their side of the story. Listening is a big advantage in the workplace, so you want to teach your child to be a good listener by being one yourself.

296. Do Not Reinforce Fearful Behavior

Fear and frustration are the hallmarks of academic failure. Many children are afraid of failure. They are afraid of the following: to put in the work that it takes to succeed, that they may never meet expectations or their goals in school and life, that they do not personally have what it takes, that someone else is better than them. There are many reasons why children could be fearful. As a parent, you do not want to reinforce fear; you want to be encouraging instead. There is no secret to succeeding and experiencing personal and professional success. The only secret is doing the work and pacing yourself without feeling stressed or overwhelmed by the work. You have to be present for your child to encourage them through their journey in school and life so that they will have no reason to be fearful.

297. Dispel Anxiety

Many parents want the best for their children. They want them to be happy and live widely successful lives. They do not want their children to be dependent on others, or the system, for their wellbeing. As a result, the fear of failure is very real for most parents. Parents worry that their children will not meet their academic goals and that they will be losers in life. This anxiety manifests itself in many ways. You may at your children too much or make unreasonable demands on your child. No matter how much you want your child to succeed, do not show them you are anxious about anything. Instead, guide them from a place of empowerment. When you are anxious, they are as well. They will not be motivated to give their best because anxiety will paralyze them and make your child feel this is about you, not them. Make this about your child's best interests, not about your fears.

298. Provide Reassurance

Your primary job as a parent is to provide your child with a comforting, empowering, and nurturing atmosphere where they can produce their best results. Provide warmth and support in the home environment where they can feel safe. Give them a space at home where they can enjoy the ability to produce their best work. A work mood, atmosphere, and environment are critical to success. Do the best you can to provide this for your child. There is a difference between providing what your child needs to be successful and going all out to make them comfortable. Your goal is not to make your child comfortable as this can have the opposite result of what you expect. Anyone who is comfortable never feels the need to try harder because they feel fine in their current state. Do not make your child feel they have it all. The goal is a suitable learning environment, not a comfortable environment.

299. Red Flags

As your children grow, they will start to take on new behaviors and traits which may surprise you. Do not be surprised to see your amazing child act out of character. Realize certain things will start to change as they socialize more with their peers. There may be some copying of behaviors which negatively impact their life. Even the best of parents, who have done everything they know to do for their children, have experienced behaviors in their children they never dreamed possible. Pastors' children have become teenage parents right under their noses! As a parent, you have to be watchful to catch the red flags. You cannot get so busy with your life that you assume your child is okay. Always be the parent who is there to communicate with their child and to know what is happening in their lives. Pay attention and talk to them if you see anything out of character.

300. Aim High

Whatever it is your child wants to do, encourage them to set big goals and aim high. Encourage them to raise their expectations of themselves, to believe if they can be a pediatrician, why not be a pediatric surgeon? Never feel you are putting too much pressure on them. If you follow successful coaches and mentors, you will learn about the power of the human ability and tenacity. As people, we are capable of doing so much more than we have ever been taught to believe. Your child can do so much more than you think. With the right vision, skills, and habits, they can reach the highest level of excellence. Remember, you are investing in a successful future for your child, so make sure they do what it takes to claim that successful future. They must constantly be thinking about their next level of greatness by aiming high.

301. Primary Job

You want your child to know their primary job right now is to learn, and through learning, to become successful in life. If your child does not see their primary job as staying focused in school and working hard to be successful, what alternatives do they have? Gone are the days when children can play Russian roulette with their lives. Even if a child decides to drop out of school with the goal of making it on their own, this is extremely risky. You will need a lot of resources and support to be successful in this way. You want to encourage your child to dedicate their time to being an excellent student and to realize that through the power of reading, they can create what they want for their lives. Even if they to decide school is not an option for them, they still need to be avid readers to be successful at what it is they love to do.

302. Prioritize Study Time

Encourage your child to designate specific times studying, and to prioritize their time. Study time is for doing homework or to study for a test or quiz; it makes a tremendous difference in a child's future and should never be taken for granted. Teach your child to see their study time as time that they can learn, grow and make a difference in their lives. It may not look that way now, but the greatest acts of human existence have been completed in very unexpected environments. During your child's study time, you want to encourage them to stay focused on the task at hand and to avoid distractions. You need to help them to see this time as a game changer in the grand scheme of their lives and not just as boring. Teach them about the power of focus and important study habits. Studying is hard work, but it is non-negotiable to academic success. In order to succeed in school, you have to study. That's the bottom line!

303. Conversations

There are certain conversations you must have with your child as they get older. Some of these conversations are about: God, money, school habits, career future, the opposite sex, drugs, self, friends. These topics are crucial because they form the core foundation of your child's wellbeing. These are issues which define your child, their identity, and their successful future. If you do not have these conversations with your child, they will have them with their friends, and those friends can give them erroneous information which will lead to your child making mistakes. You know what they say about mistakes; it is better to learn from other people's mistakes, not your own. Mistakes can be costly. Drugs, for example, will derail your child from their plans, leading to homelessness and even jail time. Often, it is enough to communicate right and wrong by exposing your child to the right environment. Take them to a good church which preaches the Word of God and they will learn to stay away from mistakes in life.

304. Let them Figure it Out

It is not always healthy to rescue your child when they encounter difficulties in completing a task. At some point, they must learn to figure it out on their own. For example, if your 10-year-old is learning to do dishes, they will probably make a few mistakes before they finally get squeaky clean dishes. Show them how to do it, but let them make their mistakes instead of taking the dishes from them and doing it yourself. If they are still learning to do the laundry, they will make mistakes before they finally get it right. Let them do the best they can, instead of intervening. When it comes to homework, give them guidelines, but let them work it out on their own. Do not be an enabler; instead, be an encourager, someone who cheers them on from the sidelines.

305. Reading Comprehension

The way students learn to read is by reading, but the way they learn reading comprehension is by thinking about what they are reading. It is possible to be reading without thinking about it; this affects reading comprehension. You can help your child develop a love of reading very early in life. The way to do this is by asking them questions before, during, and after they read. Have conversations about the book, discuss the characters, ask what the main ideas and supporting details are in the story. Ask where the story took place, and what could have happened to cause the story to have a different ending. These conversations are critical because they help them develop an authentic connection with the text and ingrain it in their minds. Reading comprehension is critical because it helps your child interact with more complicated text as they get to high school, college, and the workplace.

306. It Gets Tougher

If you think the earlier grades are hard, then you should buckle your belt and get ready for what is ahead. Middle and high school are extremely challenging, especially if your child is taking AP, honors, and community college classes. To survive and excel in their high school years, they must have the elementary fundamentals down pat. Your child needs to establish diligent work habits very early on. This will take them a long way in scaling through the tougher years ahead. If you see your child struggling, find additional help through a tutor, or establish routines at specified learning times. Understand that it will get tougher as your child advances in grades; this is a reality. They will be expected to do more challenging work which will push the limits of their determination. Prepare them for this by talking about it and setting up the right skills and mindset.

307. Make Time Count

Make the time you spend with your child count; enjoy every moment. Many parents take this very simple principle for granted. Do not be one of them! The reason we do what we do as parents is because we are thinking about our children. We work to fund their dreams and provide for them. If you do not love your child, you will not do any of this; but if you love them, you will show them by making the time you spend with them count. Create opportunities to spend time with each other and enjoy those moments. Although you may think your child loves you for the things you buy them, they care more about your love. Show that love through the moments you spend together. I guess you can say they want to have their cake, and eat it, too. Hey, it is their birthright! Who can blame them? Would you not want the best of both worlds, too?

308. Use Car Time to Talk

Your automobile should be a university, a learning space. If you are not having conversations with your child there, you should be playing audio that lifts your child's spirit either through music or narration. It is amazing how many parents drop their children off at school while blaring loud music in the car. If you are one of these parents, let me ask you: Do you ever stop to think about how this affects your child? Do you even care if this affects your child? All this loud music does is get your child's mind rattled and highly hyperactive. They come to school agitated and excited. Not only that, it shifts their thinking about what is important. They are thinking more about the music than about their school work. So, change the music or turn it down; better yet, have a conversation with your child while you are in the car together. Talk about life, ask them questions, even a simple, "How are you feeling?" will get words flowing. This is a question that makes anyone feel great.

309. Eat a Meal Together

The work week is so extremely busy that it may be challenging to find time to eat a meal together as a family. Gone are the days when families use to sit down and break bread together consistently. These days, moms and dads have to work and take care of the family while the children have to go to school. Everyone's schedule is so different it is extremely hard to get everyone in the family home at the same time. Even when a parent stays home, the child's activities may require driving to different places, at odd times, for sporting events. Mealtimes are challenging because differing schedules cause family members to want to eat at different times. Additionally, the digital world has completely changed the rules for family social gatherings. Notwithstanding, it is imperative you try to find a chance to sit down and eat a meal as a family. If this is not possible, take them out to brunch or dinner every once in a while to have your mealtime.

310. Relax Rules on Weekends

Just about every parent looks forward to the weekend. The weekend is a time to let it all go. Weekdays are extremely busy, with dropping children off at school and picking them up, running errands, running between children's activities, in addition to your agenda. Even routines at home keep everyone in the family on the edge! We are human beings; we are not machines. Our bodies get tired; every time you get an opportunity to relax, seize the moment. On the weekends, give your child a small break, let them sleep in a little. Remember, you are not the only one who has had a rough week. School work can be very challenging, so cut them some slack. You do not want to entirely excuse them from their chores and make them think they can get away with laziness (this inconsistency can hurt them in the long run), but try not to be so dogmatic about it.

311. Write Down Strengths

Have your child write down their strengths. At first, this may seem like a silly exercise, but it is paramount in helping your child see that they are a powerful being. Require them to write down all they are good at and what they like about themselves. The people who are successful are the people who believe they are talented. They have a great sense of self and a feeling of adequacy in what they can offer the world. If your child does not believe they are good at anything, they will continue to live under the shadow of doubt. They will easily feel intimidated by others, unsure and uncertain about themselves. You never want your child to have low self-esteem. You want them to believe in their strengths, but first, they must learn to identify them. Get a journal and encourage your child to write all these things down, preferably before they become teenagers.

312. Gratitude Journal

Another thing to encourage your child to write down is items and experiences they are grateful for. If you are concerned your child has a sense of entitlement, and they are selfish, you are not alone. Many parents share this same belief. The current generation has been accused of feeling entitled and thinking that everyone owes them a living. It is not their fault. We have advanced highly as a society, and things which used to be hard to come by are now easily available. The generations before us struggled to get a job, make ends meet, and have access to simple necessities to live a comfortable life. These days, our children do not have to struggle like our parents did; so much is available to them now. That being said, try not to nurture a feeling of entitlement in your child. Encourage them to keep a gratitude journal or to have an attitude of gratitude. Encourage them to be grateful for the opportunities available to them, and to never take anything for granted.

313. Family History

Your family comes from somewhere. What is the history of your family? What defines you as a people? What are the beautiful aspects of your past and your culture which you can share with your child? I am not talking about a culture that harms, denigrates and hurts others. That is not culture; It is oppression designed to keep people down. There are beautiful aspects of all cultures which enhance individuals and contribute to their emotional and physical wellbeing. What are these things in your culture? Teach your child about them. Knowing your family history gives your child a sense of identity and shows them who they are and where they come from. An identity that is rooted in a rich history and culture can help your child go a long way toward living and implementing family beliefs in their lives while enjoying a sense of belonging. A positive culture is getting lost in the current global economy, as most parents just want their children to be healthy and happy without all the extras.

314. The Less Fortunate

One of the most powerful ways to put things in perspective for your child, and to teach them gratitude, is to discuss the less fortunate in our society. Tell them about the children in the hospital who have challenging health situations. Talk to them about the children in less fortunate places around the world who have to struggle to find food every day just to live. If possible, take them to interact with these children and experience it for themselves. Many times, children take things for granted because they do not know how hard others have it. But if they have a sense of people's struggles, it might help them put things in perspective. Sit down and talk with your child; get their opinion on how they can make life easier for others or how they can live their life to show empathy for what other children may be going through.

315. Problems Build Character

Teach your child to learn from both the good and bad things that happen to them. Teach them to keep problems in perspective. Encourage them to find the lesson in each of their problems, and not be overwhelmed by them. I know finding inspiration and enthusiasm when someone has a problem is a tough thing to do. However, that is when you must decide to handle the bad things that happen to you with grace and intention. Many people truly struggle in life as a result of the problems and disappointments they have to deal with in their lives. Some people never find any normalcy after they go through a challenging disappointment. They abandon their marriages, their businesses, their children. Teach your child not to overreact when they have problems. Sometimes things will go your way, and sometimes they will not. Prepare your child to understand that disappointments are a fundamental part of life and that they grow by learning from problems.

316. You Cannot Quit

As a parent, you have a tremendous responsibility to take care of your children. It is a mandate and responsibility that never goes away. Whether you like it or not, you have to stick with it. It does not matter whether your children are rude to you, curse you, use obscene words in your presence, or are just plain naughty. You have to stay on the job and be on top of it. Being a great parent is a non-negotiable moral and legal obligation. Not only do you have to tolerate the setbacks and the exhaustive aspects of being a parent, but you also have to be at the top of your game. You have to be the best parent you can be all the time. It is a position which will come back to haunt you later in life if you do not give it the attention it deserves. The evidence will be in how your children turn out.

317. Your Attitude About School

Your child's attitude about school directly flows from your attitude and energy about school. How you stress the value and importance of education to your child will determine the level of urgency they give to it. If you are someone who is casual about school (never talk to your child about school; never find out how they are doing; never ask about their school day; never check to see their report card; never concerned about failing grades; keep them absent from school when they tell you they do not feel like going to school), and you have a non-urgent way of thinking about school, this will impact your child's learning in significant ways. Have a positive, focused, and serious attitude about school and communicate that to your child the best you know how. Encourage your child to see school as a non-negotiable aspect of their lives, leading to the amazing life that awaits them at the end of their journey through school.

318. Be Alert

It is natural to be on the alert as a parent; you always want to be certain your child is safe and doing the right thing at any given moment. Never let go of that focus. Every part of you must naturally be concerned about what your child is doing at any given time. Even when you are away, you must be able to have a sense of where your child is and be confident they are okay. We hear stories often of parents who have been on drugs and alcohol and lost track of their children. Some have even given their children away just to feed their unhealthy habits. It is unconscionable if you, as a parent, fail to take all reasonable precautions to ensure your child is on track for a prosperous future. You must always live in awareness and intention to create positive outcomes for your child.

319. Giftedness

It is a fact that everyone is born with unique gifts. Everyone comes into this world with something that they are amazing at or with a beauty that makes them the special being that they are. Discover your child's beauty, discover the aspects that make them amazing. Consistently point out what is great about them, and help them see the beauty and power that resides within them. Even as adults, there are things which we are very talented at, but we either do not know it, do not believe it, or just think it is not important to us or anyone else. As far as your child is concerned, never let them feel that they have nothing to offer the world, and never let them minimize their gifts. Encourage them to take pride in their gifts and to use them to improve their lives and the lives of others. Always be helping your child to see they are unique, they are beautiful, and they have the power to change the world.

320. Rags-to-Riches Stories

The experiences of others teach us powerful lessons about our lives. It is always exciting when we can learn and be inspired by the stories of others. If you are the parent of a dyslexic child, tell them stories of dyslexics who have gone from struggling to succeeding. If you are the parent of an autistic child, share stories of people with autism who are living amazingly successful lives. If your child struggles with ADHD, share stories of others who have surmounted impossible odds and created successful lives. If your child has a learning disability, teach them never to accept the label as something that limits or defines them. No one has the right to put a cap on someone else's ability; children have the power to rise above their current situation with the right skills, attitude, and belief systems. An important aspect of finding this motivation is reading the stories of others who have gone from rags to riches.

321. Read Biographies

The biographies of others can give perspective into our lives. It helps to read about the life experiences and stories of great people. Some of this information is taught in school history classes. If your child does not have access to this information, do research on the biographies of select people whom you want to know more about. Get books from the library, or print information from the internet and invite your child to read and discuss the stories with you. Some biographies are widely taught such as those of past presidents, great leaders who fought for rights and freedoms, very successful business owners, and more. There are so many lessons and inspirations to be drawn from the experiences of these people. For example, what shaped their views on life? What principles did they live by? What did they accomplish in their lives? What lessons we can learn from them? What do you and your child find inspiring about them?

322. Success Habits

Habits are extremely important in the pursuit of any worthy goal. If your child does not have success habits, school and life will be very difficult. As a student, there are certain critical habits your child must keep. They must have the habit of waking themselves up every morning, so you do not have to. They must have the habit of waking up on time, of doing their homework and studying every single day (preferably at a specific time and in a specific, quiet location), of writing down the things they plan to accomplish for the day, and of checking things off the list as they accomplish them. They must have the habit of going to bed on time, of limiting their phone use to specific times of the day, and they must have specific learning habits when they are in class, such as listening, engaging, and being focused. Practicing these success habits now will lay the foundation for reaching long-term goals and a bright future.

323. Being Successful

Hopefully, as a parent, you are familiar with stories of successful people. My hope is that someday you want your child to be one of those people. You want them not just to survive in life, but to live extraordinary lives and be highly successful. If this is true for you, then you have to study what other successful people have done. Find out what habits they implement on a daily basis to catapult themselves to success. These habits may include waking up very early in the morning to get started with their day. They do not sleep past mid-day because they understand the value of time. They keep a to-do list because they are extremely busy and have several things they desire to accomplish. They also exercise. Ironically, average people say they do not have time to exercise, yet the busiest individuals in the world make time. Success takes discipline, focus, consistency, and hard work!

324. Manage Your Time

One of the most important aspects of keeping your sanity as a parent is staying organized and managing your time wisely. You cannot look at your day as one big chunk of time that you can shove everything into and make it fit. Doing so causes you to run around like a chicken with its head cut off. Have you seen parents who run around frantically wanting to do everything at once? You need to be more organized than that and handle your parenting business with grace. Break up your day based on what you want to accomplish – a to-do list comes in very handy for this. Prioritize your list and do not do things that are not a top priority, at least not right away; move them to the next day if necessary. For other things, just say no. You must learn to say no sometimes so that you do not take on too much responsibility which will cause you to burn out.

325. Mental Exercises

We have talked about the importance of physical exercise, but mental exercises are also ideal for your child. The ability to keep their brain active and alert is just as important. One of the most important ways to keep your child's brain active is to play games, crossword puzzles, or word searches. Not only do these games keep them focused for a given period, but they also help to build their cognition and reasoning skills. These games also help your child strengthen their vocabulary. Many of these games are readily available on the internet. You can also get some books from the store at a very affordable cost. Games provide an opportunity to bond with your child as you play with them. Do the best you can to provide your child with this opportunity. You will be giving them a powerful skill, mindset, and ability that will help them for the rest of their lives.

326. Be Honest About Money

Personally, I think real authenticity comes from honesty and accepting your situation, no matter how bad it looks to others. Telling the truth about your finances to your child is something that you and other parents may disagree on. Most parents would rather just pretend that they can afford things when they cannot. They go into debt to purchase their child what they want, even if they clearly know they do not have the money. My philosophy is to tell your child the truth when you cannot afford to buy something for them. Just say, "I would love to get you this item but I cannot afford it right now." Or, you may choose to tell them you do not make enough money. What is wrong with that? Use it as a teachable lesson and say you do not want them to be like you. You want them to be able to make a lot more money than you when they grow up and not have to experience the same struggles as you.

327. The Golden Rule

Teach your child the golden rule, which is to "treat others as you want them to treat you." The Golden Rule builds character and strength without compromising your child's self-worth. There are so many people who think only about themselves; they are very selfish and do not think about how their actions affect someone else. As a result, they do things which harm others emotionally and physically. They do not show empathy for how others feel and carry on as if the world revolves around them. This attitude probably started when they were young, and it went undetected or uncorrected. As a parent, you want to make sure your child feels empathy and treats people like they want to be treated. You cannot assume your child will do this on their own. Each time you see them exhibit an act of selfishness, use it immediately as a teachable moment to correct them.

328. Respect Begets Respect

To get respect from your child, you have to treat them respectfully. Being a parent does not give you permission to be rude, insensitive, or bossy. Give the same courtesies to your child that you would give to anyone else. It does not make any sense to be nice to others, yet not be nice to the people who are closest to you. When this happens, it is because the parent takes their children for granted. You always assume since you see them every day, that they will always be around and always love you. With a stranger, you want to make a good impression, so you try harder to be nice. This should not be! You need to give everyone the same courtesies and never take your loved ones for granted. Your child will learn to be courteous to others if you are courteous with them. Remember that communication and respect are critical in the 21st-century workplace, so teach your child the basic skills of interacting with others by demonstrating them yourself.

329. Respect Your Child's Privacy

Many ordinary people have skeletons in their closets. You probably do, too! It is likely that your child has moments of needing privacy which they would like you to honor. Respect your child's privacy; do not sneak into their room to snoop around or look through their personal belongings (unless you have reason to believe their safety may be in jeopardy). I am confident you will feel a bit awkward if you do this, and you know you will be in big trouble if your child catches you, too. Seek to establish and nurture a more trustworthy relationship with your child. Ask yourself, "Why does my child feel the need to hide something from me?" It could be because you have not been open enough with them; it could be you are judgmental, and they know you will not agree with their views and opinions if they ask you.

330. Difficult Homework

As your children progress in grade level, they may begin to experience some challenges with homework. These challenges may introduce frustrations which may cause them to experience an academic setback. I know you do not want this to happen to your child. You need to implement some simple homework strategies which will help them get through the challenging times. You first want to make sure that they are keeping up with their homework daily, and doing it in a very quiet environment without distractions. You also want to be sure they have had something to eat, and that their minds are well-rested. Finally, ensure that they begin with the most difficult homework problems first, while their brain is alert and able to process information more accurately. Encourage and motivate your child through their challenging assignments and reassure them that you understand the challenge. Teach them to be patient with the process and to see the value of it all.

331. Trust and Safety

Be overly cautious about who you allow to spend time with your child. Not everyone has your child's best interest at heart. Not every friendly face is friendly. Picture yourself in a scenario where you had to go to work and decided to leave your child with your boyfriend/girlfriend, totally trusting they would take care of them. However, you later find out they have been harming your children in your absence. My first question would be, why? Why would anyone leave their children in the hands of someone they do not know very well? Nothing is worth the risk of exposing your child to danger. Your first instinct as a parent should be to protect your child. Nothing is more important than your child's safety If you expose them to danger, they may never forgive you. You may also cause an emotional scar which may not heal, even when they are an adult.

332. Early Start on Projects

Procrastination is a bad habit that will negatively impact your child's grades. Make sure you are keeping them on top of their homework, and that they complete it before it is due – preferably as soon as they receive it from the teacher. It is important to finish it early to avoid feeling rushed as the due date approaches. If your child waits too long before starting the work, it will be nearly impossible to invest the time it takes to fully research, plan, and complete the task in an organized way. It is always a good idea to plan enough cushion before the assignment is due so that if there are any errors your child can fix them before turning the work. Always to encourage your child to implement good study habits so they can be motivated to complete their work early.

333. Competitions

There are many resources and activities that your child can participate in at school. Increasingly, schools are offering enrichment activities which provide students with skills that go beyond content and curriculum. Encourage your child to take part in these activities. There are also inter-class, inter-school, and inter-district competitions that your child can get involved in. Some of these activities are spelling bees, math bees, writing contests and essays. If there is a possibility for your child to take part in these based on their skills, then by all means let them participate. You are building their muscle for future competition on the job. You are teaching them how to prepare for an important presentation and how to develop the stamina to handle a challenge. Encourage them to practice before the competition and to give it their best shot. Tell them to take it seriously and to spend a lot of time studying for it. Even if they do not win, they gave it their best, and that is what counts!

334. Book Collection

There is never anything wrong with books. Seek opportunities to provide books for your child, and keep many books in your home. You may not have the funds to purchase books for your child, but there are tons of books in schools and at libraries. Ask the school principal about book sales where you can make purchases at very affordable prices. Make book acquisitions a priority in your parenting. If you cannot bring the books home with you, take your child to the library and let them read there. You can also take your children to bookstores and let them experience and interact with books there. The good news is you do not have to be a special kind of parent to give your child these experiences with books; it does not cost you anything. Instill a love of books in your child and the long-term benefits will be enormous.

335. Invest in Books

You may not have the funds to buy many books for your child, but you could get that one book which would make a tremendous difference. Have the mindset to invest in books. Understand that when your child's mind expands as a result of the things they read, this will be a game changer for their lives. You should never consider it a waste of money if a book causes your child to think and see things in a unique and expansive way, or if a book helps your child develop critical thinking. It is never a waste of money when your child loves to spend time reading books they enjoy and learning new things. Buying books is an investment in your child's creative genius and your child's future because it broadens their thinking. So find out from your child if there are any books they love reading and want to own, and invest in books.

336. Managing Devices

Cellphones and devices pose a challenge for every parent. Even when their children know how to handle these devices in their lives, most parents are concerned that their children may let these devices distract them and cause them to lose focus. This is a genuine concern. The truth is, many students struggle in school, not because they are not smart, but because they let these devices get in the way of what is truly important in their lives. The idea is not to completely yank these devices from your child's life, but to talk to them about how these devices can affect them if they do not use them the right way. Encourage the productive use of cell phones. Encourage your child to use their phones to do research, to communicate with peers during group projects, to check on a friend to see how they are doing, to phone their parents and check in. Devices are not exclusively meant for social interaction and talking about things that add no real value to their lives.

337. Story-Telling

When your child reads a story from a book, encourage them to interact with the story and with the text. You do this by asking them questions about what they just read, such as what happened in the story and why, what might happen, and what they would do if they were in the position of any of the characters. By putting themselves into the story, they feel and experience what they are reading. This exercise is crucial for young readers who are building their reading and comprehension skills. You will have to be patient with the process initially, but it creates a solid reading foundation very early on, which will take them a long way as they move up in grade levels. Sometimes, even older children will come to you to talk about a book they are reading and how interesting it is. Take time to discuss it with them. Ask about other books they are reading. The key is to listen.

338. Milestones

It is true every parent has to work extremely hard to support their family and provide food, clothing, and shelter for their child. It is also true that being present provides emotional support for your child. Part of being present for your child is celebrating their milestones and accomplishments. You may have a very hectic work schedule or other activities which keep you busy, but you need to make an effort to be present during crucial moments in your child's life, from recitals to high school graduation, competitions to sporting events, or whatever is important to them. If your child invites you to an event, do your best to be there for them. Children grow up fast, and before you know it, they will be on their own, and you will not have these opportunities anymore. Bosses come and go, but children will always be with you. Your boss will probably not even notice you missed a meeting, but your child will remember if you miss their first recital.

339. Control Your Temper

You may have a temper problem which your parents did not help you with, but you certainly cannot allow that to flow into your parenting life. If you have a temper problem, seek help and learn to control it. Never let your temper flare at your children. Can you imagine how scared and horrible they feel when you yell at them because you are angry? If it is done once in a while, it is normal, but if your daily parenting involves yelling, scolding, screaming and being angry, then you need to seek help. Try to be as reasonable and as calm as possible when you express your expectations to your child. You do not want your children to fear you or think you are mentally unstable. You need to be taken seriously, so find a balance between being firm and being loving when correcting your child.

340. Stand United with Your Spouse

If you have a spouse, make sure you are both in accord as far as discipline is concerned. Your children must see you as a united front and understand that they cannot pit you against each other. They should not be able to manipulate either of you; they *will* try to find the weakest link. If you find that you are not strong enough to say no, defer to the other spouse. Never let your child get away with something, or tell them not to tell your spouse! Doing so teaches your child to lie, gossip and lose face with the other parent. Never let your child feel that you are "better" than the other parent. You should always work together as a team to solve problems that involve your child. This approach is better for you and will make your life a lot easier. You will not have to worry about implementing things on your own.

341. Criticize Behavior, Not the Child

To avoid tearing down your child's self-esteem, be sure you are criticizing their behavior (or their actions), not them. When your child manifests a behavior which you think may take them off-track from their goals, talk to them about it. Never say they are an awful child for doing the action. State that such action is unacceptable and suggest alternatives. Instead of addressing your child with statements such as, "you are bad," or "you are a mean person" or "you are very selfish," focus on their actions by saying, "it was wrong not to share with your sister," or, "sharing is caring." Explain why the behavior is wrong and how doing it will affect them or someone else negatively. Do not point out behaviors in a blaming way; be stern, be firm, but also be kind. Do all correction in a private area, not in public.

342. Enforce Rules Consistently

When it comes to applying rules you have established as a parent; it is important to be consistent. The first step is setting the rules; you may, or may not, want to seek your child's opinion on this – it will depend on the rule, your child's personality, and their age. Once you have established a rule, you need to enforce it on a consistent basis. Your child may attempt to manipulate the rules or make excuses as to why it should not apply this time, but it would be a huge mistake on your part to change the rule even once. If you change it once, then you may change it again, and then you will have to explain to your child why you are not changing it this time when you changed it last time. The best way to avoid this is to apply the rule firmly and never change it in the middle of the game. If you find yourself saying, "okay, but only once," then you give your child permission to attempt to break the rule again. Stand your ground until your find that the rule no longer applies.

343. Sex, Alcohol, and Drugs

It is never too early to start exposing your child to subjects such as sex, alcohol, and drugs. If you do not talk to your child about these things, someone else will, and they may even find out through personal experience. You do not want that! These three things always lead children astray. Your child can end up pregnant and with disease; homeless and on drugs; or in prison with a DUI. Let them know they need to wait until they are older and wiser so they can make informed decisions and avoid falling under the influence of people who do not have their best interests in mind. Have the kind of relationship where your child can come to you and talk about anything without fearing your reactions or judgments. You do not want them to make horrible mistakes which will ruin their life forever.

344. Use Online Resources

The beauty of technology is the availability of resources. There are many resources online which your child can use to complete their homework. Encourage them to use a search engine, such as Google, for research. If they find themselves stuck during homework, suggest they use the many online resources and tools available on the internet. Many teachers give out lists of resources to students. A popular one for math and science is Khan Academy. YouTube also had videos which teach how to solve math problems and do science experiments. Honestly, there is no reason for a child to struggle in school if they have the patience to work through the information at their disposal. The real problem is they would rather be doing something else with their computer instead of using it in a way which benefits them academically. Staying focused on completing homework is critical to ensuring their grades stay up, and that should be important enough for them to use the tools available to complete the work.

345. Let Your Child Help You

If you own a business or have any side job which you do, involve your children. Assign them roles so they can work with you. If you are a speaker, take your child with you when possible, to sit at your table to collect sign-ins. If you are a mechanic, take your child to your shop and give them a small, safe job to do. If you are a doctor with your own practice, take your child to your clinic and give them a job. (Be sure to check your state laws in regards to privacy and safety before allowing your child to work with you.) It is crucial to involve your child in what you do because it teaches them responsibility. You are helping them to use their time wisely by being productive and learning a trade. This also teaches them empathy and helps them experience what you have to deal with to support them. Children need to understand the effort which goes into work. You are also teaching them to start thinking about future jobs.

346. Teach Consequences

Children need to know there are consequences for their behaviors. Hopefully, you can raise your child in such a way that they are responsible, well-behaved children who do not need to learn consequences the hard way. This is entirely possible if you implement the principles taught in this book. In the event you do have to teach them, make sure they know there are unpleasant consequences for improper actions and behaviors. Never let your child get away with anything – not even one bad behavior. If they can get away with one, they will repeat it and think it is acceptable. Teach your children that wrong-doing cannot go unpunished. If you have to, take their phones away, put them in time out, or say no to something that they love. Make sure that you do this in love and tell them why you are doing it so they understand their actions are unacceptable.

347. Decisions

Let your child make their own decisions sometimes. You can guide them in the right direction without imposing your will on them or telling them what to do. Although you may feel that your child is not listening to you, they probably are. The principles and foundations you taught them will go a long way toward helping them make sound and reasonable decisions. At some point as adults, your child must think for themselves, so let them practice when they are young. Some mistakes can be costly; you want to protect your child from bad decisions. Be observant; find a balance between letting them make decisions on their own and not letting them make mistakes that could harm them in the long run.

348. Accountability

When your child does something wrong, hold them accountable for their actions. Teach them to fix their mistakes. If for example, they are playing ball and break the windshield of a neighbor's car, you must require that they pay for it or at least contribute something toward fixing it. You want your child to understand they cannot get away with doing whatever they feel like doing. If their school work is not complete, they may have to sacrifice some of their free time to get their work done. If their chores are not getting done, they must be held accountable and required to finish them. Accountability teaches your child that when they commit to doing something, they have to follow through to the end to be sure it is complete. They need to learn to honor their word and to take responsibility for their actions. In so doing, they are learning to hold themselves accountable.

349. Talk Through Difficult Situations

In this world, stressful situations will happen that have the potential to topple your family life and cause enormous heartbreak for you and your children. Think about how you would want to address situations like these with your children. Sadness is such a personal issue; it is hard to tell someone how to feel and how to communicate those feelings with others. As far as your child is concerned, you always want to talk about difficult situations with them in a way that leaves them whole. You do not want them to feel depressed and so sad that they can hardly carry on with life. One great approach is to ask how they feel about the situation. You will be very surprised how mature children can be. They will sometimes say things that impress you. Capitalize on their ideas and help them find the lessons in the setbacks. Tell them the good things that come from a painful experience and what lessons they can take from that.

350. Give up Your Vices

We have talked about being a role model for you child. For some parents, that may be asking too much. If you cannot be a role model, you can at least make an effort to protect your children from your vices. Smoking in the presence of your child puts their life at risk of second-hand smoking which is linked to many respiratory problems in children. Not only is this harmful for your child, but it could also be lethal for you as a parent. Do you not want to live to see your children grow up to be responsible, productive human beings? The same goes for alcohol and drugs, which might expose your child to violent, irritable and unpredictable behaviors. Imagine being a child and living in such an unstable environment. Imagine how fearful you would feel waking up to this every morning. Model responsible behavior for your child, and avoid unhealthy vices that put their lives in jeopardy.

351. Mainstream Parenting

Do not be inflexible in following parental stereotypes and principles of your culture, family, race or ethnic group. If you live in a dogmatic society and feel your life is at risk if you do not implement these principles, then, by all means, please be safe. However, if you live in a progressive society where you are free to make your choices, then choose to raise your children to freely express their creativity without feeling constricted by cultural norms and values. There is more than one way to raise a child. Parenting is an emotional, personal, and instinctive experience. No one has your child's best interest at heart the way you do. Cultures are more focused on limiting behaviors to ensure society continues to flow in one way. That may not be your desire for your child. Encourage your child to freely express their creative genius without the limiting expectations of culture.

352. Teens Need Love Too

A teenager who is on the brink of adulthood needs the support of their parents, now more than ever. Many parents of high school students think their children are grown and independent and no longer need them. They turn over some parenting decisions to school counselors and rely on them to make educational choices for their children. However, your child needs your help during these years, more than ever. This is when they start to make serious decisions about careers and love relationships. Do not think just because they are a little older that they can figure it out on their own. Granted, some children believe they know it all. Do not give up! Continue to be alert and step in when you can to give them advice, but do not be overbearing or intervene unnecessarily. Give them room to think their issues through and they will always come to you for opinions. Be that presence which is always there when they need you.

353. Your Love Interests

If you are a single parent, you may have love interests. Address your desire to be loved, but remember this rule: your children's interests and needs come first before your own, or anyone else's needs! Do not abandon your child for your love interests. When you are dating, make your child a priority. Do not expose your child to danger by bringing someone new into the household that you do not yet know well. People hide behind masks and can wear those masks long enough to get what they want. Do not be naïve in your thinking! Your child needs to feel you are defending them, and your biggest priority is to ensure they are safe and loved. If you are tending to the needs of a new potential partner and start leaving your child out and do not address their needs, your child will grow to resent your new friend and you. They will feel abandoned and insecure. You need love in your life, but it should not come at the cost of your child's emotional health.

354. Budget

Teach your child basic budgeting principles. A budget is an estimate of income and expenditure for a set period. Your child needs to learn not to spend more than they make and to live within their earnings. Spending more than you make/have means that you are operating in a deficit. This is a dangerous place to be, and that is how so many people get into debt and find it difficult to come out of debt. You want to help your child create a budget so they can manage their money wisely. Each month, encourage them to account for money that will be coming in and going out, based on their earnings, needs, and wants. Teach them about long-term and short-term saving. This is an excellent way for them to learn about making room for incidentals and unforeseen circumstances, and how you must plan ahead.

355. Earn an Income

Give your child ideas on making money, even if it is just pocket change. Some parents choose to pay their children for chores. That is certainly an option if it teaches your child the principle that they must work to earn money. But children also need to learn that being a family means we all do our part to make the home run well, and they will not get paid for that. There are creative ways your child can earn money around the house, like doing odd jobs (washing the car, cleaning the baseboards, etc.). If they are older, they can babysit, help a sibling with homework, or sell items online. These are fantastic ways to develop entrepreneurial skills in children. As one who advocates academic excellence, I do not believe children should work outside the home during the school year. If your goal is to prepare your child for a long-term career, getting a job may be a distraction.

356. Enjoy the Rhythm of Life

Take time to enjoy the rhythm of life with your child. As busy as you are, find a chance to serenade yourself in your surroundings. Children learn through exploring the environment around them. They are fascinated by flowers, birds, animals, sprinklers, soil, and outdoor beauty. Do not rush the process of exploration. Let their imagination run wild while you are outside. For children, this is such a welcome relief from the world of TV and computer screens which cause them to be depressed, obese, hyperactive and have behavioral problems due to watching these unstable devices all day, every day. Do your child a favor by taking them outside to breathe in clean, fresh air. Outdoor activities help children think outside of the box and learn new ways of seeing solutions. Being outdoors also helps children enjoy some basic childhood needs like screaming, hiding, observing worms and experimenting with stones. Let your child be free as you sit there and watch the wonders of their imagination.

357. Unreasonable Expectations

As much as you want your child to succeed and be the amazing human being you know they can be, try not to place unreasonable expectations on them. When your child feels pressure to do things that are not in alignment with who they are, it will cause them to struggle. As they seek to find themselves, they will feel frustrated between doing what is in their heart and doing what pleases you. A child's life is filled with so many pressures from teachers, counselors, friends, society; they are overwhelmed by so much already. Try to help them set reasonable goals and organize their time so they can achieve what they need to achieve to succeed. Encourage your child to meet their full potential, but do not let fear of failure cause you to have anxiety about how your child will turn out or if they will succeed. Do not let how your own life turned out, or what you would have wished for your own life, be a deciding factor of what you expect from your child.

358. Trusting Others

Be overly cautious about who you allow to spend time with your child. Not everyone has your child's best interest at heart. If you cannot leave your child at a public daycare, then you must investigate thoroughly the person you entrust to care for your child. Never make a decision that puts your child in harm's way. People are not always who they claim to be. Any harm done to your child could affect them for the rest of their lives. You will live with the guilt of not ensuring that your child is in good hands, with a trustworthy person. While you may have an urgency that requires you to be away from your child, always think of their safety; make it a priority. Nothing is more important than your child's safety. Let that be at the back of your mind when making a decision about who to trust with your child.

359. Be a Good Mother

As a mother, your greatest joy is to see your children succeed in the world. Remember that your love will make a tremendous difference in their lives. The world should never underestimate what you do for your child because you live, breathe and sacrifice every day to see that they become all that you envision. It is unthinkable and gut-wrenching to see your child go down the wrong road in life. As a mother, you want to be supportive of your child's dreams, aspirations, and hobbies. If they do take the wrong path, look at yourself in the mirror and ask what part you may have played in causing this to happen. Do not get angry and take things personally, but be patient and find your calm before expressing your displeasure to your child. Do not be pushy and insist on having your way. Find a nice balance between helping your child and making sacrifices. Always be approachable; be a good listener when your child comes to you to talk. Work with your spouse to make parenting easy.

360. Be a Good Father

Being a good father, like being a good mother, is not easy. You must be present as a father. You need to be a fair disciplinarian, a good role model; try to sympathize with your child's needs without imposing your will on them. You may be the breadwinner in the family, but as much as possible, be present for your child. Love them and show them you care. Be there for the important moments in their lives, such as college graduations, sporting activities, and marriages. Children often remember the special things their fathers tell them, so think of profound life lessons that your child can live by to shape their life for the better. Plan to go on trips with your child and take the time to create a stable relationship with them. Let them see your personality and be influenced by the good things in you. Whatever you do, do not get violent.

361. Be Careful in Love

You may need love in your life but do not bring someone new into your home that you do not know well. Do not be so emotionally vulnerable and needing love to the point that you are willing to compromise your child's safety to meet your needs. People are often not what they pretend to be, so take the time to get to know someone you think you love. Give yourself several months or years to grow into a relationship before you decide if this person is worth introducing to your children. Many children are harmed daily by adults who come into their homes as "friends." Make it a rule that your child's needs come before your own. Although you may feel you love someone and they love you, give yourself time. If they truly love you, they will wait until you are ready. Do not be so needy of someone's love that you rush to make things happen before you know all about them.

362. Bullying

Talk to your child about bullying and its tell-tale signs, such as when someone belittles them, puts them down, or is always telling them what to do. Behaviors such as those can escalate if they are not addressed promptly. Teach your child never to let anyone intimidate them or make them feel awkward. Encourage them to speak to you about their feelings. Talk to them about types of intimidation so that when it happens, they can immediately identify it for what it is. Also teach your child not to bully others. Teach them empathy and the golden rule; teach your child to put themselves in other people's shoes and to treat others the way they want to be treated. Truly, bullying has no place in our lives. We make the world a better place by respecting each other and encouraging the growth of others. It starts with one parent, one child, one home!

363. Believe in Your Special Needs Child

As human beings, we are each born with our unique abilities. No one person is exactly like someone else, and they should not try to accomplish what someone else can accomplish in the same way. We each come with our unique abilities based on our emotional, mental, and physical realities. This means we improve our lives based on the vantage point from which we start. The same goes for your special needs child. If you try to compare your child with the abilities of others, it will only frustrate you. Take your child for who they are and work with them from that vantage point. Expose them to resources, skills, habits, and principles that will build them up. Believe in the incredible potential of your special needs child. What can you do to support them in doing more of what they can do? What are your visions and goals for your child? Where do you see them in the future? Implement practices and beliefs that take them there.

364. Acknowledge Struggle

One of your biggest goals as a parent is to identify when your child is struggling with something emotional or physical. Be observant and always check-in with your child to see how they are feeling. Be aware of when your child is having a hard time. Maybe your child is struggling because they have a lot of school work and do not know where to begin. Maybe your child is struggling with rejection from a friend. Try to understand your child's distant, subdued, or emotional behavior. Have a friendly chat with them about what is going through their hearts, minds, and heads. Put yourself in your child's shoes and imagine how you would want someone to support you if you were going through something similar. Be understanding but also make sure your child is not just making an excuse for a bad decision; keep them accountable for their actions but acknowledge their struggle.

365. A Parent's Work is Never Done

Understand that you will always be a parent no matter how old your children are. As long as you have children, you have work to do. There is a natural tendency to be on alert as far as your child is concerned. You always feel a natural instinct to want to step in and support them, even when they are older. How you raise your child will have a life-long effect on them; one day, you will reflect on your life's work and either give yourself a pat on the back or feel regret. Hopefully, if you applied everything you have learned in this book, you will look back with pride and a smile on your face. When they are older, you will not always be a constant, daily presence in your child's life, but you must always do and say things which lead them to believe you love them unconditionally, care about them, and will always be there for them, no matter what. Children who are raised well and love their parents will return to them for advice and still find relevance in what they say. Remember that! Your point of view will always matter to them!

ABOUT THE AUTHOR

Dr. Nicoline Ambe is a professional speaker, educator, and #1 best-selling author. She has taught in several elementary schools, colleges, and universities across Canada and the United States for the past two decades. She holds a bachelor's degree, two master's degrees, a Ph.D. in Law, as well as a California teaching credential. She is a #1 best-selling author of four books - _A Teacher's Notes_, _Above & Beyond_, _Innate Genius_, and _The Big 7 Talk_. Dr. Ambe has made numerous public television and radio appearances. She has been featured in several online publications. Through teaching, speaking, and training, Dr. Ambe has helped many parents develop great relationships with their children, resulting in academic excellence. A significant part of her mission involves teaching children to recognize their talents, stay focused, develop a learning mindset, and succeed in school.

Dr. Ambe has spoken in front of several large audiences from coast to coast. She is available to deliver keynotes, presentations, and training at schools, conferences, conventions, schools districts, churches, and events.

To learn more about Dr. Ambe, visit: **www.nicolineambe.com**

More Books by Dr. Nicoline Ambe

A Teacher's Notes: *Helping Parents Prepare Their Children at Home for Success in School.*

Above & Beyond: *How to Help Your Child Get Good Grades in School and Position Them for Success In College, Career, and Life*

Innate Genius: *A 31-Day Student Guide to Being More of Yourself and Achieve Outstanding Results*

The Big 7 Talk: *Crucial Subjects That Every Parent Must Discuss with Their Children*

Parenting Day by Day: *365 Tips for Raising Bright and Goal Driven Kids*

www.nicolineambe.com/books

STAY IN TOUCH

Website – www.nicolineambe.com
Facebook – www.facebook.com/ambenico
Twitter – www.twitter.com/nicolineambe
Books – www.nicolineambe.com/books
Newsletter- www.nicolineambe.com/newsletter

DID YOU LIKE THIS BOOK?

Please take a minute **to leave a positive review** of this book on Amazon! Your feedback will help me continue to publish books that help you get results.

~ *THANK YOU* ~

Made in the USA
San Bernardino, CA
21 February 2017